Phil Maggitti

Pugs

Everything About Purchase, Care,
Nutrition, Behavior, and Training

Filled with Full-color Photographs
Illustrations by Michele Earle-Bridges

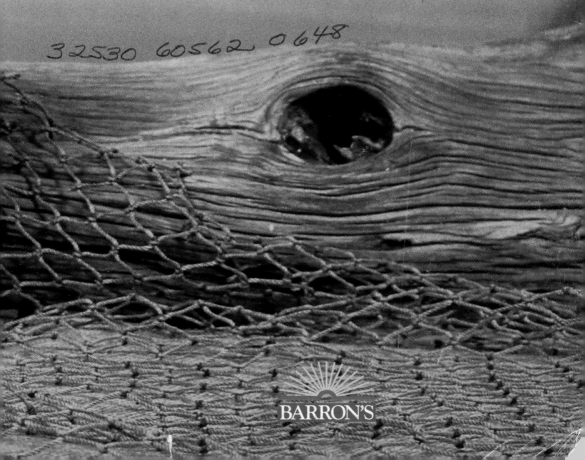

BARRON'S

2 CONTENTS

A FEW WORDS ABOUT PUG HISTORY

The first recorded appearance of the word *pug* in the English language occurred in 1566. *Pug* was a term of endearment then, applied to persons but rarely to animals. By 1600 *pug* had acquired two additional meanings: "courtesan" and "bargeman." These would appear to be strange bedfellows, linguistically at least, but *pug* did not stop there in its acquisition of new themes. By 1664 *pug* also meant "demon," "imp," "sprite," "monkey," and "ape."

Not until the middle of the next century, according to *The Oxford English Dictionary* (OED), did *pug* come to mean "a dwarf breed of dog resembling a bull-dog in miniature." The OED also added that the pug "on account of its affectionate nature [was] much kept as a pet." So much so that in 1749 David Garrick, an English actor and theatrical manager, wrote, "A fine lady . . . keeps a pug-dog and hates the Parsons."

Monkeying Around with Definitions

Some disagreement exists regarding the manner in which *pug* came to be applied to these endearing, impish, spritelike, solid-as-a-barge, sometimes demonic little monkeys that were great favorites at court if not with cour-

The word "Pug" was born in the sixteenth century as a term of endearment applied to people but seldom to animals.

tesans. Many observers believe that *pug* first was applied to monkeys, and, after certain facial resemblances between monkeys and the little dogs with the curly tails had been noted, the word was applied to the dogs, too. (This application was noted as early as 1731 in England.) Persons subscribing to this theory point out that pugs were called *pug dogs* originally to distinguish them from pug monkeys.

Other observers wrote that *pug* was derived from the Latin *pugnus,* meaning "fist," because to some people the Pug's profile resembled a clenched fist. Still others believe pug is a corruption of Puck, the name of the mischievous fairy in Shakespeare's *A Midsummer Night's Dream.* The puckish nature of the Pug would seem to support this theory, but the OED does not. After acknowledging that *pug* "agrees completely in sense with Puck," the OED cautions that *pug* "is not easily accounted for as a mere phoenetic variant" of Puck.

Like so many questions regarding animal history, the matter of how the Pug got its name—and how that name eventually came to be written in some contexts with a capital *P*—in the end devolves to a no-one-can-be-certain resolution. Our money is on the borrowed-from-the-monkey-name theory; but before we leave this question, we should point out that *Pug* also has been applied to lambs, hares, squirrels, ferrets, salmon, moths, small locomotives, foxes, trout, clay, and the footprints of any beast. Anent the capital *P*, this convention is followed in books about dog breeds and in other breed-related contexts, but in civilian writing the only words capitalized in breed names are proper nouns that would be capitalized in any context.

No Dutch Treat

Although no one knows for certain when or where the Pug arrived in Europe, the Dutch are usually credited with being the agents of the Pug's importation. Called the *Mopshond,* a Dutch word for "grumble," the Pug was greatly favored as a lap warmer by Dutch ladies, who stayed cozy in their large, unheated houses, we are told, by placing a Pug or two on their laps.

The Dutch are also credited with introducing the Pug to England. This glorious event is commonly alleged to have occurred in November 1688 when the Dutch prince William III of Orange and his wife, the English princess Mary, landed at Torbay in South Devonshire to ascend the English throne. According to virtually all Pug historians and authors, by the time William III and his Pugs arrived in England, the Pug had been anointed the official dog of the House of Orange in the Netherlands.

The breed owed this status to the heroics of a Pug named Pompey, who had saved the life of William III's grandfather, Prince William the Silent. The governor of Holland and a fancier of Pugs, William the Silent left the Netherlands for Germany in 1567 after Philip II of Spain had sent an army to Holland to put down an armed revolt that had arisen the year before. Unwilling to remain silent forever, William led a counteroffensive against the Spanish army in 1572. One night during that campaign, as

William lay sleeping in his tent at Hermigny, assassins approached. Pompey began barking and scratching in an attempt to warn his master. Finally, he leapt upon William's face to alert him to the approaching danger. Consequently, wrote Sir Roger Williams in 1618, "untill the Prince's dying day [1584], he kept one of that dog's race; so did many of his friends and followers."

"That dog's race" was described by Williams as "a white little hounde," but most observers concluded, as did Susan Graham Weall, author of *The Pug,* that "it can reasonably be thought, from other parts of its description, that it actually was an ancestor of the modern Pug." The other part of the white little hounde's description that seems to have convinced Weall and others of Pompey's pugnacity was Sir Roger's report that Pompey and others of his ilk had crooked noses called camuses. That, we are told, clinches the argument because *camus* is a French word meaning "flat-nosed" or "pug-nosed." Moreover, the likeness of a Pug dog lies at the feet of William I's effigy in Holland's Delft Cathedral.

Recently, however, convincing information that refutes these claims has been presented by Robert Hutchinson, a research scientist at the American Museum of Natural History and the author of *For the Love of Pugs.* "At first blush," writes Hutchinson, "the cumulative effect of this mass of circumstantial evidence would seem to confirm beyond a reasonable doubt the argument for the Pug" being a great favorite in the House of Orange and the savior of William the Silent, not to mention Protestantism the religion. Nevertheless, continues Hutchinson, closer inspection "discloses a house of cards" in the House of Orange accounts.

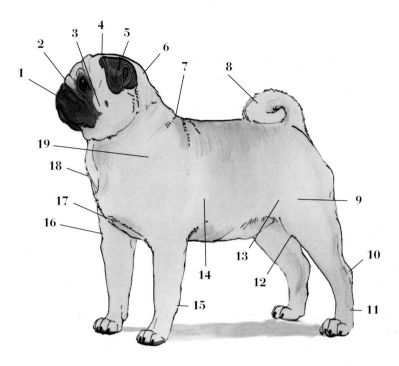

The anatomy of a Pug:
1. *muzzle*
2. *stop*
3. *cheek*
4. *skull*
5. *ear*
6. *crest*
7. *withers*
8. *tail*
9. *hindquarters*
10. *hock*
11. *metatarsus*
12. *stifle*
13. *loin*
14. *ribcage*
15. *pastern*
16. *forequarters*
17. *chest*
18. *brisket*
19. *shoulder*

The first joker in the deck is the effigy of William I in the Delft Cathedral. Citing personal reports from several Dutch dog fanciers, Hutchinson argues that the dog at William's feet in the cathedral is a *Kooikerhondje.* This small white hound with bright orange markings is little known outside of Holland, but inside Holland the *Kooikerhondje,* not the Pug, is "universally credited" with saving William I. Insiders also report that the Kooiker was the mascot of the House of Orange. In further support of this contention, Hutchinson cites additional popular and some scholarly evidence.

In a Dutch-made television biography of William I, a Kooiker was cast in the role of William's canine savior; and in *Nederlandse historien,* first published in 1642, the Dutch historian Pieter Corneliszoon Hooft credits a *Kooikerhondje* named Kuntze with saving William's life.

Hutchinson also points out that the English word *camus* meant something quite different in Sir Roger Williams' time than the French word *camus* does today. The latter is admittedly a synonym for "pug-nosed," but that meaning did not come into existence until the nineteenth century. In Williams' (and William's) time, the English word *camus* was used to designate a nose that curved upward or downward, not a nose that was resolutely marching toward the back of its owner's skull.

In his measured, entirely convincing brief, Hutchinson further asserts that there is "no documentary evidence from the seventeenth century to indicate that the Pug was an Orange mascot." What's more, "Dutch art of

the seventeenth century reveals no images of Pugs at all." Finally, "there appears to be no hard contemporary evidence of the presence of Pugs in England prior to 1730."

The Pug, says the American Kennel Club standard, "is an even-tempered breed, exhibiting stability, playfulness, great charm, dignity, and an outgoing, loving disposition.

Continental Favorites

The Pug's popularity was not confined to England and Holland. The low-slung rascal had friends in high places throughout the rest of Europe, too. One of the Pug's greatest champions in France was Josephine Bonaparte, wife of the emperor Napoleon. Josephine's Pug, Fortune, bit Napoleon on the leg when he was climbing into bed on his and Josephine's wedding night in 1796. Fortune survived that

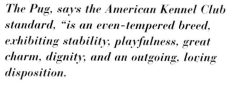

A house is not a home unless there's a Pug in it.

Hearing, seeing, and speaking no evil, three young couch-potatoes-in-training.

encounter, but he did not survive a challenge to the cook's English Bulldog. Following this misfortune, the pugnacious little Pug was replaced by another one, also named Fortune. When the unfortunate Josephine was imprisoned at Les Carmes, Napoleon sent love notes to her hidden in Fortune II's collar.

The Pug dog comes equipped with its own advertising slogan, **Multum in parvo,** *a Latin phrase that means "a lot of dog in a little space."*

The Pug was also well known in Italy and Spain during the eighteenth century. In 1789 a Mrs. Piozzi wrote in her journal, "The little pug dog or Dutch mastiff has quitted London for Padua, I perceive. Every carriage I meet here has a pug in it."

A painting by Goya places the Pug, or *Dogullo* as it was called, in Spain by 1785, and the use of the word *Mopsorden* (Order of the Pug) by German Masons, who were excommunicated by the Pope in 1736, serves to date the Pug in that country.

The Pug Dog's Origin

Questions about the Pug's origin, like questions about the derivation of its name, elicit more nobody-knows-for-certain answers. Most authorities agree, however, that the Pug is an Oriental breed, whose common forebears are the Pekingese and the lion dog—the ancestor of today's Shih Tzu—and whose country of origin is China. Like all other dogs, the Pug ultimately descended from the wolf, a special variety of lap wolf, no doubt, that was waited on hand and paw by the other wolves.

Estimates of the time at which the Pug originated are varied: before 400 B.C., says one observer; in 600 B.C., says another; more than 1,800 years ago, says a third. This uncertainty is occasioned in no small part by the Emperor Chin Shih, who destroyed all records, scrolls, and art relating to the Pug sometime during his dynasty, which lasted from 255 to 205 B.C.

As others would do who would know and love the Pug in later centuries, the Chinese had several names for Pugs, including *Foo* or *Fu* dog, Lo-Chiang-Sze, Lo-Chiang, Pia dog, and Hand dog. The Chinese also were known to send animals as gifts to important individuals in Korea and Japan. Thus, the Pug arrived in those countries during the seventh and eighth centuries.

TIP

Pugs in Black

Black Pugs, at least one researcher believes, were developed in Japan in the late ninth or early tenth century. From there the black Pugs' spread to other parts of the world mirrored that of their fawn relatives. Some of the earliest black Pugs and, hence, some of the earliest fawn Pugs—and even the occasional modern-day fawn Pug, if the truth be known—were decorated with patches of white in their coats.

The Pug in America

The first Pugs imported to the United States arrived shortly after the Civil War. The breed was one of fifteen recognized by the American Kennel Club (AKC), which was founded in 1884, but after a promising start in this country Pugs were overshadowed by longer-coated toy breeds such as the Pekingese and Pomeranian. From 1900 to 1920 only a handful of breeders were working with Pugs, and many shows drew no Pug entry at all. In 1915 the AKC registered only thirty-two Pugs, and in 1920 that number dropped to five. At that point the Pug ranked fifty-one out of fifty-eight breeds then recognized by the AKC.

Illustrated Standard

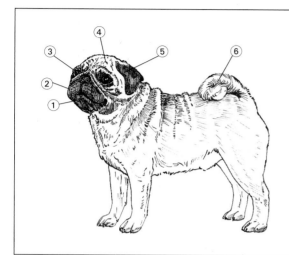

1. Slightly undershot
2. Short, square muzzle
3. Large, prominent eyes
4. Massive, round head
5. Thin, small ears, either rose or button
6. Tail curled as tightly as possible over hip; double curl preferred

❏ **Color:** silver, apricot-fawn, or black, with black muzzle or mask, ears, cheek moles, and trace down back

❏ **DQ:** none

The first Pug dog club in this country was started in 1931, but that club did not last much past its first show, which was held in 1937. In the early 1950s the Pug Dog Club of America, the parent club of the breed, was founded. Whether by coincidence or calculation, the Pug enjoyed its first popularity surge during the 1950s. Indeed, the breed more than quintupled its annual registrations with the AKC between 1950 and 1960, soaring from 958 new registrations—and thirty-first place on the AKC hit parade—to 5,080 registrations, and seventeenth place out of 106 breeds.

The Pug suffered a reversal of fortune during the next two decades, and by 1980 had slipped to fortieth on the AKC list. Pugs have pulled themselves up by their registration slips in the meantime, and in 1998, when 21,487 new Pugs were enrolled with the AKC, the breed ranked seventeenth out of 146 breeds.

All Pug breeders and, consequently, all Pug dogs are not created equal; but, unfortunately, there are no intelligence or integrity tests required of persons who breed and sell dogs. The phone number you dial to inquire about puppies may lead you to a conscientious, compassionate individual motivated solely by the love of this breed and the desire to contribute to its ongoing perfection. You may, on the other hand, find yourself talking to a craven opportunist who would sell a puppy to a band of devil worshipers as long as they paid with a certified check or postal money order.

Sorting out the good, the bad, and the awful breeders is not difficult, however. If you approach a breeder's house and the odor makes your eyes begin to water as you near the front door, do an about-face and try another breeder. Conversely if the look of the breeder's dwelling suggests that the crew from *House Beautiful* is due any minute, and there is no evidence that a dog, much less a puppy, has ever set foot in any of its rooms, keep looking until you find a house that appears more dog-friendly.

Even though temperament and good health are heritable to a greater or a lesser extent, the way a puppy is raised is usually more important in shaping his personality and in determining his state of health. Puppies that are not handled often enough between the ages of three and fourteen weeks are less likely to develop

This little creature looks as if he was on the other end of the line when E.T. phoned home.

into well-adjusted family members than are puppies that receive frequent handling and attention during this time. Therefore, you would do well to ask how many litters a breeder produces each year and how many other litters he or she was raising when the puppy in which you are interested was growing up. A breeder who produces more than three or four litters a year, or who was raising two or three other litters while your puppy's litter was maturing, may not have had time to socialize every puppy in those litters properly. A breeder who raises only two or three litters a year—and preferably not at once—has more opportunity to give each of those puppies the individual attention he deserves. In general, the smaller the "kennel," the more friendly the puppies it will produce and the more healthy those puppies will be.

Where to Find a Pug

Breeders

A conscientious breeder who raises a few well-socialized litters a year is an excellent source for a Pug. Such dedicated individuals may advertise in dog magazines, in the classified sections of newspapers, on bulletin boards in veterinary offices, in grooming shops and feed stores, and in *Pug Talk,* a publication no Pug lover should be without (see Information, page 92). Prospective buyers also can meet Pug breeders by visiting dog shows, which are advertised in newspapers, veterinarians' offices, dog magazines, and, occasionally, on television.

Pet Shops

Anyone who considers buying a Pug from a pet shop should ask the pet shop owner for the name, address, and phone number of the dog's breeder. If the pet shop owner is unwilling or unable to provide that information, the buyer should proceed with caution because he or she is proceeding with less information about the puppy than normally would be available if the puppy was being purchased directly from the breeder.

If the pet shop owner provides the name and address of the puppy's breeder, and if that person lives nearby, the prospective customer would do well to visit the breeder to observe the conditions in which the puppy was raised. If the breeder lives far away, the prospective buyer should telephone to ask questions about the puppy, such as:

✔ How many other puppies were in the litter?

✔ How old was the puppy when he left his mother?

✔ How many dogs does the breeder have?

✔ How many litters do those dogs produce in a year?

✔ How many different breeds of puppies does the breeder produce?

✔ Why does the breeder choose to sell to pet shops rather than directly to the public?

In addition, the prospective buyer should call the humane association in the town where the breeder lives to ask if the breeder enjoys a good reputation in that community.

Recommending this sort of caution is not to insinuate that buying from a pet store is, per se, always more risky than buying directly from a breeder. What is implied, though, is that the buyer should find out as much as possible about a Pug's background no matter where that dog is acquired.

Animal Shelters

Difficult as it may be to believe, some people, through no fault whatsoever of their Pugs, do not get along with their dogs. In such rare circumstances the unworthy owner should return the Pug to his breeder, who, of course, will take the dog back promptly, find him another, more suitable home, or keep the dog forever—as all reputable breeders do without fail or hesitation.

Nevertheless, some Pugs do wind up in animal shelters with their tails tucked, as far as they can tuck their tails, between their legs. If you are willing to wait for a Pug until one is surrendered at a shelter near you, present yourself at the shelter and ask to be put on its waiting list. No matter how long you have to wait for a Pug to arrive at the shelter, your patience will be rewarded, and a special place at the table in Pug lovers' heaven will be set for you.

Breed Rescue Clubs

While you are visiting the shelter, ask if there are any Pug rescue clubs in the area. Members of rescue clubs often cooperate with shelters by providing foster homes for lost, abandoned, or surrendered Pugs, feeding and caring for them while trying to locate suitable new owners.

Questions to Ask Yourself

Male or Female?

Some people, because of personal inclination or prior experience, prefer the companionship of male or female dogs, but given love, a supply of things to chew, and a place on the bed at night, either sex will make a fine companion. The cost of spaying a female Pug is $30 or so more than the cost of neutering a male. Otherwise there is no difference in the expense associated with housing an altered male or female—and no difference in the amount of care each requires.

Puppy, Adolescent, or Adult?

If Pug puppies were any more appealing, they would be illegal. What they lack in brainpower they make up for in curiosity. What they lack in experience they make up for in exuberance. They stomp joyfully through their food bowls and their days, tails wagging, heads lolling, eyes shining, bellies and hearts overflowing.

Pug puppies do not consider anyone a stranger and with luck they never will. They stir us to laughter, reduce us to baby talk, and summon from us a tenderness concealed beneath the armor we wear in our daily confrontations with life. Small wonder that long-term relationships between Pugs and their owners often begin with a terminal case of puppy love.

The adolescent Pug, while slightly less manic, is just as appealing as his neonate self. We acquired our first Pug, a neutered fawn boy named Percy, when he was nine months old. If he had better moves as a puppy, I'm sorry I missed them.

Percy was chauffeured from Florida to Pennsylvania in late January 1991 by a professional dog handler returning from the Florida winter circuit. We arrived at the handler's house with a crate in the back of our Geo Storm hatchback. After we had put Percy into the crate, my wife returned to the house to get her purse. I said idly, "Well, Percy, how's it going?" and the little chap nearly came out of his skin. He began to bark, whoop, and whine and hop up

and down, pawing at the bars of the crate until I thought he was going to declaw himself. I opened the crate, and he fairly leapt into my arms, still in the throes of a ten-plus turn-on because I had known his name.

When my wife returned to the car, I returned Percy to his crate. He was still so excited that he peed all over the crate before we got to the end of the driveway and was obliged to sit on my lap the rest of the way home. If a puppy could top that whirling dervish performance, I'd like to make that puppy's acquaintance.

The adult Pug, too, remains young at heart; and just as the adolescent Pug is not much different from a puppy, an adult is not much different from an adolescent. Indeed, it is difficult to determine where adolescence leaves off and adulthood begins with Pugs.

Our two youngest Pugs, Burt and Harry, are almost three years old at the time of this writing (June 1999), and they show no signs of approaching or even contemplating adolescence, much less adulthood. Their maternal grandmother, Patty, and her litter sister, Ella, who are now seven, were equally rambunctious at the same age. They do not play with quite the same manic dedication the boys exhibit these days, but their enthusiasm for the finer things in life—marrowbones, rides in the van, harassing the dog next door—is no less keen than the younger dogs'.

Fawn or Black?

A Pug's physical characteristics are governed by genes, the coding units that transmit genetic instructions from an individual to his or her offspring. Genes, as you remember from high school biology, are arranged in pairs on chromosomes, and each gene occupies a specific

address (or site) on a chromosome. That address is called the gene's *locus* (plural, *loci*).

Each member of a pair of genes can occur in different forms, called *alleles*. At the color loci in a Pug, for example, there can be an allele that tells the coat to be all black, or an allele that tells the coat to be fawn with black ears and mask. The allele for black is dominant. Thus, a Pug will be black if he inherits one black allele and one fawn allele—or two black alleles. Consequently, there is only one or two alleles' difference between a black and a fawn Pug, and the choice between a black and a fawn is, essentially, a matter of aesthetics.

One Dog or Two?

Pugs are also adept at amusing members of their own species, once those members have come to accept the Pug's presence. If you are

Pug puppies are all eyes, ears, innocence, alertness, and enthusiasm.

acquiring your first puppy, you should think seriously about acquiring two, even if there is always someone at home during the day and your puppy will not have to spend great amounts of time alone. In addition to human company, puppies should enjoy the company of another dog that will always be interested in romping and stomping long after humans have tired of the game, and that will always be more willing to let another dog use him for a pillow than a human is.

If you already have a dog and that dog is still of flexible age, preferably five years old or younger, it is not too late to add a second dog to the household, providing you manage the

A person's brain could go into vapor lock at having to choose just one puppy from such an engaging clan.

introduction properly (see Introducing Other Pets, page 35). Before you do, though, you should consider certain realities.

Two dogs are not as easy to keep, feed, clean, and look after as one; nor, in some cases, will you simply be doubling your workload by adding a second Pug. That load can increase geometrically, not linearly, depending on the personalities of the dogs involved and the amount of mischief they inspire in one another. But—and this is a significant *but*—

Whether dressed for the opera or a weekend in the country, the Pug is always sartorially correct.

whether or not your workload increases by a factor of two, three, or six, the pleasure that two dogs provide is always more than twice as great as the pleasure that one can give you.

If you are going to add a second dog—or acquire two dogs at once—you have to decide which of three configurations is going to be most conducive to peaceful coexistence: two males, two females, or one of each. Again, opinions vary. One owner will say that two males, after they've been altered, will get along better than a male and a female will. Others say that a male and female make a better choice, even though females do tend to dominate males. Still others recommend getting two females. If you're getting two Pugs at once, the breeder(s) of those dogs should be able to help you in this regard. If you already have one dog and you're adding a Pug to your family, the sex and temperament of your present dog should be the guiding criteria.

If buying a second Pug would tax your budget, adopt a dog—one that is roughly the same age and will grow up to be roughly the same size as the Pug you are purchasing—from a local shelter. Of course, when you adopt a dog from a shelter, you should follow as much as possible the same guidelines you would follow when purchasing one (see The Puppy Checklist, page 19).

Many breeders of pedigreed dogs imply—and others assert—that one cannot have as much confidence in a shelter dog's personality as in a purebred's. That belief is questionable. Because shelters take in far more animals than they can place, most shelters screen their dogs thoroughly and euthanize any that are not sound physically or emotionally. Your chances of getting a nonquality dog from a shelter are no greater than they are of getting one from a breeder. Indeed, as Joe Stahlkuppe has observed in *Keeshonden*, another breed manual in this series, "For every responsible dog breeder who will help you find a good puppy there are several others to whom only your money is a motivation."

Show Dog or Pet?

Unless you are planning to show and/or breed, you want a pet-quality Pug. Pet quality—an unfortunate and disdainful-sounding term—is used to designate dogs with some cosmetic liability that argues against their breeding or showing success. Pet-quality Pugs may have muzzles that are too pinched, noses that are too prominent, tails that are not as tightly curled as a show dog's, or some other "fault" or minor constellation of faults. None of these surface defects in any way detracts from the Pug's sterling personality, for every Pug is a quality dog at heart.

If you want to throw your hat, your Pug, and your money into the show ring, make that desire clear to the breeder when you go to look at puppies. Many first-time dog owners who cared not a whit about showing when they brought their pups home suddenly become flushed with pride in their dogs and mistakenly assume they are show prospects simply because they are pedigreed. Pedigrees, however, do not show dogs make. In fact, most pedigreed dogs are not show quality—if show quality means good enough to earn a championship.

If, after buying a Pug at a pet price, you are suddenly inspired to begin writing to show superintendents for entry forms and premium lists, let the dog's breeder know what you are interested in doing, then ask if you can take the dog to the breeder for an evaluation. If you bought your dog from a breeder who lives far away, ask a local breeder to evaluate your dog. An ounce of prevention can be worth a pound of disappointment in the show ring.

How Much Is That Doggie?

The price of a Pug is determined by age, quality, supply, demand, and geography. Very young Pugs, twelve weeks old or so, are generally priced between $500 and $1,000, depending on the breeder's assessment of their potential. A $500 puppy, though his topline may not be correct and his chest might be a little narrow, will make a lovely companion if he is healthy and properly socialized. The same is true of a $1,000 puppy, which has been priced higher because his breeder feels he has some show potential. Puppies with a lot of show potential—as much as this determination can be made at such a young age, which is not much at all—are not usually available because their breeders want to see how they develop.

The Age of Consent

Puppyhood is one of the special joys of dog owning. Dogs are dogs their entire lives, but they are puppies for only a few precious months. Thus, new owners are eager to take their puppies home as soon as possible. Be that as it may, responsible breeders do not let puppies go until they are between ten and twelve weeks old. By that age a puppy has been weaned properly, has been eating solid food for several weeks, and has begun to make the transition to adulthood.

Puppies that are younger than ten weeks old are still babies. Take them away from their mothers and their siblings at that age, and the stress of adjusting to new surroundings may cause puppies to become sick, to be difficult to housebreak, or to nurse on blankets or sofa cushions, a habit they sometimes keep the rest of their lives. No matter how tempting a

CHECKLIST

The Puppy Checklist

✔ Eyes—bright, glistening, and clear

✔ Nose—cool and slightly damp

✔ Gums—neither pale nor inflamed

✔ Ears—free of wax or dirt

✔ Body—smooth, perhaps a little plump, but not too skinny

✔ Coat—free of bald patches, scabs, or specks of black dirt

✔ Hindquarters—free of dirt or discoloration

• A puppy with teary eyes may be in poor health, especially if his nose is dry or feels warm.

• Inflamed gums may indicate gingivitis; a puppy with pale gums may be anemic.

• Wax inside his ears may simply be a sign of neglect; but if his ears are caked with dirt, the puppy may have ear mites.

• If a puppy's ribs are sticking out or if he is pot-bellied, he may be undernourished or he may have worms.

• A puppy with a dull-looking coat or one dotted with scabs, tiny specks of dirt, or bald spots may have ringworm or fleas.

• A puppy with wet hindquarters may develop urine scalding; if they are dirty, he may have diarrhea. Both urine scalding and diarrhea are signs of potential poor health.

"Nature teaches beasts to know their friends," said Shakespeare.

He followed me home, honest!

seven-week-old puppy might be, he will adjust better if he is allowed to remain in his original home until he is several weeks older.

Basic Personality Tests

The basic personality test for puppies is simple: Any puppy that comes racing over to investigate you as soon as he sees you is a good bet to make a swell companion. If you desire a more discriminating test, simply wiggle a few fingers along the floor about 6 inches (15 cm) in front of the puppy, or wave a small

toy back and forth about the same distance away. Does the puppy rush to investigate? Does he back away in fright? Or does he disappear behind the nearest chair?

Well-adjusted, healthy puppies are curious about fingers, toys, and anything else that moves within sight. Nervous or timid puppies, or those that are not feeling well, are more cautious. Poorly adjusted puppies head for cover.

If you have other pets or children at home, the inquisitive, hey-look-me-over puppy is the best choice. The bashful puppy might well make a fine companion, too, but he may take

Winsome, adj., sweetly or innocently charming; winning; engaging (see also, "Pug").

longer to adjust, and is, perhaps, better left for experienced dog owners who currently are without pets or young children. And the little one behind the chair? Shy puppies need love also. Plenty of it. If you have no other pets or if you plan to acquire two puppies at once and have the time and patience required to nurture such a reluctant violet, God bless you. If not,

perhaps the next person who comes along will be the right owner for this needful pup.

Contracts and Papers

Breeders should provide a sales contract when selling a puppy. Most contracts specify the price of the puppy; the amount of the deposit required to hold the puppy, if any; when the balance of the payment is due; and so on. Contracts also may specify that if at any time the buyer no longer can keep the puppy, or no longer wishes to keep him, the breeder must be given an opportunity to buy the puppy back at the going rate for puppies or dogs at that time.

Note: A contract specifying that the breeder be allowed to buy the puppy back at the original price would most likely not hold up if challenged.

Finally, a contract should specify that the new owner has a definite period of time, usually three to five working days after receiving a puppy, in which to take him to a veterinarian for an examination. If a veterinarian discovers any preexisting conditions such as luxating patella or a heart murmur, the buyer should have the right to return the puppy at the seller's expense and to have the purchase price refunded.

Deposit

When buyers give a breeder a deposit on a puppy, they should write "deposit for thus-and-such puppy" on the memo line of the check. They should make a similar notation when writing a check for the balance of the payment. Buyers should be given receipts for all payments, and they should find out in advance—and in writing if they wish—whether a deposit is refundable should they decide not to take the puppy. Buyers also should remember that once a breeder has accepted money or some other consideration in return for reserving a puppy, the parties of the first and second parts have entered into an option contract, and the breeder cannot legally revoke or renegotiate the offer, as some breeders may try to do, if the puppy turns out to be much better than the breeder had anticipated.

Buyers are advised to read a contract meticulously before signing it because contracts are legally binding once they have been signed by both parties. If a contract contains any stipulations that buyers do not understand or do not wish to agree to—like a stipulation saying that the dog must be shown to championship—they should discuss these issues with the breeder before signing.

In addition to the pedigree, new owners usually receive "papers" when they buy a pedigreed dog. These papers usually consist of a registration slip that the new owners fill out and send, along with the appropriate fee, to the administrative office of the American Kennel Club (AKC). The AKC then returns a certificate of ownership to the new owners.

Persons buying a dog or puppy that already has been registered by his breeder will receive an owner's certificate. There is a transfer-of-ownership section on the back of the certificate that must be signed by the breeder and the new owner. Once the required signatures are present, the new owner mails the certificate, with the appropriate transfer fee, to the AKC, which sends back a new, amended certificate of ownership to the new owner(s).

Health Certificates

Health certificates and vaccination and deworming records are the most important documents that accompany a puppy to his new home. Do not accept a puppy without these papers, and be sure that the health certificate you receive with your puppy was issued by a veterinarian within ten days of the time you receive your puppy.

Some breeders, especially those that produce a large volume of puppies, try to save money by giving vaccinations themselves. There is nothing illegal about this practice, yet there is more to immunizing a puppy than drawing vaccine into a syringe and pushing the plunger. Few, if any, breeders are capable of examining puppies as thoroughly as a veterinarian can before administering vaccinations. This examination is important because vaccine given to a sick puppy will do more harm than good. Thus, a puppy should be seen by a veterinarian at least once before he is sold, preferably before his first vaccination.

Why You Should Alter Your Pug

The chief reason for altering a Pug is simple—by doing so you are doing your Pug a kindness. By spaying a female before she has a chance to go into heat, you reduce her risk of contracting cancer of the uterus and/or mammary glands by 90 percent. Neutering a male before his hormones have a chance to drive him into a breeding frenzy greatly reduces his risk of contracting testicular and prostate cancers.

Altering a dog is also a kindness to yourself and your family. Altered dogs make more civilized companions. Unneutered males are wont to lift their legs to anoint vertical objects with urine as a means of marking territory and attracting females. They also are inclined to make sexual advances at your guests' legs and to regard any other dog as a potential mate or sparring partner.

Unspayed females, for their part, generally come into season (heat) twice a year. This condition is accompanied by swelling of the vulva, staining of the rugs, and, quite frequently, unannounced visits from neighborhood dogs that leave their calling cards in the herb garden. A heat lasts twenty-one days, on average,

and they will be among the longest twenty-one days you ever endure.

There are socially responsible reasons for altering your Pug, too. Although breeding an attractive, mannerly dog can provide joy, satisfaction, and the feeling of achievement that accompanies any creative activity, there is enormous responsibility incurred when that activity involves creating a life. Too many puppies are produced by irresponsible people who are looking to feed their competitive egos, turn a quick profit, or let their children observe the miracle of birth. Better they should take their children to an animal shelter and let them observe the underside of that miracle: the euthanasia of homeless dogs that invariably go to meet the needle with their tails wagging. There is no more gut-wrenching sight in all the negotiations between animals and humans.

With millions of healthy dogs being destroyed annually for want of responsible owners, the decision to bring more puppies into the world is not one to be made lightly. For all but a few people it is not one that should be made at all. The pet overpopulation problem cannot be solved by the unrestricted breeding of puppies. The number of dogs killed in shelters each year argues for restraint and common sense on the part of humans, especially those who call themselves animal lovers.

When to Alter Your Pug

Most veterinarians recommend that females be spayed when they are about six months old and that males be neutered when they are seven to ten months old. At these ages sexual development is nearly complete, but undesirable traits—urine marking by male dogs, for example—have not become habits.

LIFE WITH A PUG

Next to acquiring a Pug—and telling all your friends about your wonderful new dog—shopping for supplies is one of the great joys of being a Pug owner. That joy is compounded by the staggering variety of merchandise available to the person who wishes to provide his or her new Pug with the trappings of the good life. Never has so much been available so readily from so many sources, including pet shops, dog-show vendors, pet-supply warehouses, Internet web sites, and chichi boutiques. The possibilities are limited only by your determination and your credit-card balance.

Shopping Advice

Food and lying in a heap are the Pug dog's ruling passions. This breed's colossal appetite is legendary. For most Pugs if the subject is food, the answer is yes. In fact, Pugs will often say yes to items that are outside the traditional food groups.

One afternoon when I was in the puppy nursery about to take a three-day-old puppy's temperature, the phone in my office rang. When I returned to the nursery, which also doubles as our bedroom, there was our neutered fawn boy, Percy, with his head under the bed and his butt in the air. I assumed the same position to see what he was about.

The dark engraving in the middle of a Pug's forehead was known as a "prince mark" long before that singer fellow came along.

He was about an inch and a half into the Vaseline jar I must have knocked to the floor when I went to answer the phone. He looked as if he had greased his face in preparation for a long-distance swim. I removed the jar from Percy's eager embrace, and after checking the label to make sure he wouldn't have to be rushed to the hospital, I went back to taking the puppy's temperature.

About 10:30 that night Percy leapt from the bed and quit the room at an agitated pace. We ushered him outside promptly. He looked much relieved after a few minutes, but one spot on our lawn had suffered such an environmental insult that we feared nothing would ever grow on that spot again.

Food for Thought (beginning on page 45) contains a brief treatise on canine nutrition. Armed with knowledge served up in that chapter, the cautionary tale of Percy and the Vaseline, and the superhuman willpower needed to resist your Pug's blandishments whenever she sees you with something to eat, you should be prepared for the lifelong exercise in discipline that will be needed to prevent your Pug from becoming overweight.

Food bowls and water dishes ought to be made of metal or ceramic. Reusable plastic can retain odors even if it is washed carefully. Disposable plastic is a burden on the environment. If you choose a ceramic bowl, make sure it does not contain lead, which can be poisonous to dogs.

Whatever their construction, all food bowls and water dishes must be solid and heavy enough not to tip over easily. They should also

CHECKLIST

Shopping List for New Pug Owners

✔ Food
✔ Food bowl
✔ Water dish
✔ Place mat
✔ Collar or harness
✔ Lead
✔ Crate
✔ Brush
✔ Nail clippers
✔ Styptic powder
✔ Dog bed(s)
✔ Toys
✔ Baby gate(s)

have rubber guards on the bottom to prevent sliding. Finally, food bowls and water dishes ought to be sturdy enough not to break, crack, or chip if a dog knocks them over.

Place mats, whether fancy, decorator vinyl, or plain utilitarian rubber, will protect the carpet or floor under food bowls and water dishes. That is no small consideration if your Pug is the type that eats as though she were bobbing for apples.

Collars and harnesses are available in nylon or leather. A leather collar is fine for most adult Pugs. Sturdy nylon mesh collars, which are less expensive, are a better choice for puppies, who will need several collars while they are growing up. Because Pugs are susceptible to respiratory difficulties if they become overheated, their collars must never be tight. You can check the fit of a collar by inserting two fingers between the collar and your Pug's neck. If your fingers fit easily but snugly, the collar is properly adjusted. If you have to wedge your fingers in to make them fit, get a larger collar for your Pug, or let this one out a notch or two.

Warning: Never put a choke chain, which sometimes is fatuously known as a check chain, on a Pug.

Some Pug owners prefer to use a harness rather than a collar for walking their Pugs because a harness does not put any pressure on a dog's windpipe. Lead training is easier with a collar, however, so a harness usually is reserved for Pugs that are lead-trained already. Whether she is wearing a collar or a harness, your Pug should wear her license and identification tag whenever she leaves the house.

The lead (or leash) may be made of leather, cotton, or nylon. Some nylon leads are retractable, permitting you to keep your Pug close by when necessary or to allow her to range more freely in open spaces.

The crate is the new Pug owner's best friend, next to the new Pug, of course. Crates provide a feeling of security for Pugs and their owners. Until your Pug is housebroken, any time she cannot be with you, she should be in her crate (see Crate Training, page 30).

The crate you buy should be large enough to accommodate your Pug when she is grown, but small enough so that she will feel cozy in it when she is a puppy. A crate that measures 24 inches (61 cm) long, 21 inches (53 cm) high, and 19 inches (48 cm) wide meets those requirements. The bottom of the crate should be covered entirely with a soft mat equipped with a washable cover.

Grooming tools should be on every Pug owner's shopping list because grooming should be a part of every Pug's routine. Pet-supply shops, mail-order houses, many veterinary offices, vendors at dog shows, and some Internet sites carry the brushes, combs, shampoos, nail clippers, powders, ointments, sprays, and supplementary accoutrements necessary for keeping your Pug well groomed. Routine Care and Grooming, which begins on page 37, contains advice and instructions for using these implements to best advantage.

Dog beds are to Pugs what canvas is to an artist. The well-appointed house, therefore, contains a number of beds in which a Pug can display her talents for resting. These beds should be deployed in rooms in which you spend a lot of time. This arrangement allows your Pug to combine two of her favorite activities: sleeping and being near you.

Dog beds are available in many sizes, colors, materials, and designs, but square-cut or pear-shaped, round or oval, bean bag, thinsulate, or medical-grade polyfoam, the most important characteristic of a dog bed is a removable, washable cover.

Toys can be found in a brilliant array, artfully designed to provide hours of pleasure for your Pug; yet fun is not the sole criterion used in selecting toys for a dog—toys must be safe as well. Balls with bells inside should be sturdy enough so that a dog cannot get the bell out and swallow it. Before buying a toy for your Pug, try to imagine how the toy could cause harm. If there is any chance that it could, do not buy it.

Baby gates, the sturdy, hinged, swing-open kind, are essential for those rare times when you want to confine your grown, housebroken Pug to a room in which you are not present.

Puppies, as we have mentioned, are best left in their crates when you cannot be with them.

Pug-proofing Your House

Pugs are built for comfort, not speed. Although they should be able to jump onto a sofa or a bed easily enough, they are not great leapers, and they are, for the most part, not so tall that they can stand on their hind legs and seize food off the kitchen table. Thus, Pug-proofing your house consists mainly of keeping objects that you do not want chewed at an altitude where your Pug cannot reach them.

✔ If there are any rooms you do not want your Pug to investigate, keep the doors to those rooms closed.

✔ If there are fragile objects in the rooms your Pug is allowed to visit, put them out of reach.

✔ Make sure all sliding glass doors are closed securely and are marked in some fashion so that your Pug does not go charging into them.

✔ Make sure all electrical cords are intact.

✔ If your dog or puppy begins chewing on electrical cords, wrap them in heavy tape or cover them with plastic tubes, which you can buy in an auto-supply shop. Until you are certain your Pug has not developed a taste for electrical cords, unplug all appliances that are not in use if necessary. To keep your Pug from getting a charge out of electrical sockets, cover them with plastic plug-in socket guards, which you can buy at a hardware store.

✔ Keep all kitchen and bathroom cleansers, chemicals, cleaners, and toilet articles in cabinets that can be closed or locked securely.

✔ Keep the lids on all trash receptacles tightly closed. Consider replacing trash containers

whose swing-open lids could be dislodged if your Pug overturns the containers.

✔ Put sewing supplies and yarn away when you are finished using them.

✔ Do not leave rubber bands, hot irons, cigarettes, plastic bags, or pieces of string or yarn lying around.

In short, you must learn to think like a Pug. Look for any potential accident—tinsel on a Christmas tree or a dangling tablecloth—waiting for a Pug to make it happen.

Welcoming the Newcomer

You have bought every item on your shopping list and a few extra items as well. You

We should comfort Pugs for being dogs just as they comfort us for being human.

have set up the crate and dog bed(s). You have made a final safety check of the house. Now it's time to bring your new Pug home.

If you are unfortunate enough to have to work during the week, schedule the homecoming for the start of a weekend or vacation. Remember that even though you have planned carefully for this day, it will come as a surprise to your dog—and as a major surprise to a puppy, who will be leaving her mother, playmates, people, and the only home she has ever known.

"Basket case?! What basket case? Who are you calling a basket case?"

Most puppies adjust swimmingly. They enter their new homes with wiggly excitement and great curiosity. Other puppies (and older dogs) may not be so self-assured. Do not be surprised or insulted if your newcomer looks apprehensive. Keep the welcoming party to a minimum, and reassure your new friend by stroking and speaking to her gently. After she has taken the measure of your household, she will become more at ease, but that process should be accomplished one room and one or two family members at a time.

Your handsome and admiring Pug puppy— don't leave home without it.

Until your Pug learns what is chewable and what is not, electrical cords should be wrapped in heavy tape or covered with plastic tubes, which can be bought in an auto-supply shop.

Your Pug will feel more comfortable in her new home if she has something from her former home on hand: a favorite toy, a blanket or bed, or a favorite food. These items give off familiar, comforting smells that are reassuring in a strange, new world.

Crate Training

The greatest security blanket you can give your new Pug is a crate, and you should introduce her to the crate during her first hours in the house. After you have socialized with her for a while and have given her a chance to eliminate outdoors, place her in her crate with an interesting toy or treat. Leave the door open and stay in the room.

Helpful Hint: To establish their Pugs' attachment to the crate, some owners feed them their first meal in it.

After your Pug is used to sitting in her crate with the door open, latch the door the next time you put her in the crate. Stay in the room for a minute or two tidying up or going about any sort of normal activity, then let her out of the crate and tell her what a good dog she is.

Once your Pug is used to the idea of staying in her crate with the door closed, leave her alone in her crate for a minute or two, then return to the room and let her out of the crate, telling her what a good dog she is. Your Pug will learn to be relaxed about your comings and goings if you treat them matter-of-factly yourself, starting with the crate-training process.

As you teach your Pug to stay in her crate for progressively longer periods, you are preparing her to use it as her bed and safe haven, her own private wolf den. A dog will not soil her bed unless she is nervous or in dire straits. Thus, creating positive associations toward the crate will enable you to use it as an aid to house-training and as a secure place for your Pug when you cannot supervise her.

For the first few days after you bring your new Pug home, however, you should keep her near you, even if this means placing the crate in one part of the house during the day and moving it to your bedroom at night. This will do much to ease your Pug's adjustment to her new home.

House-training Without Tears

House-training a dog is simple. It consists of knowing that your dog has to relieve herself before she knows it. Fortunately, this is almost as easy as it sounds. If you understand a puppy's behavior patterns, she can be house-trained with minimal difficulty.

The younger the Pug you acquire, the less likely she is to be house-trained, but no matter how young she is, she ought to have been paper-trained by her breeder. Paper training begins when a puppy is about three weeks old, the age at which puppies start to eliminate spontaneously. At this point a breeder puts newspaper at one end of the cozy, blanketed nest the puppies share with their mother. Young as they are, the puppies will take themselves to the newspaper most of the time when they have to eliminate. This is how puppies, who are born with an instinct to eliminate away from their nest, get the idea that newspaper is an appropriate surface for elimination.

This idea is reinforced when puppies are old enough to start romping around out of the nest—at four to six weeks of age—but not old enough to go outside yet because they have not been vaccinated. By spreading newspapers over a large area of the puppy nursery during playtime, the puppies' breeder encourages them to continue using the paper for conducting personal business.

Going Outside

If your Pug is not house-trained when you get her, you will have to take her out-of-doors several times

A Pug's crate is his home within a home, a sanctuary to which he can repair when he wants to stop and think or when he merely wants to stop.

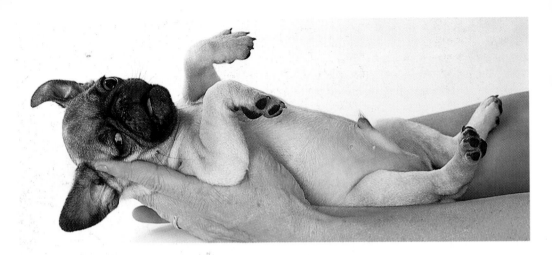

a day to the spot where you want her to eliminate. The first trip out should occur immediately after the puppy wakes up in the morning. Make sure she has urinated and defecated before you take her in for breakfast, and make sure you praise her as if her delivery were an envelope with Ed McMahon's name on the outside, declaring you a sweepstakes winner.

Pugs are a tactile as well as a visual delight, as much fun to hold as they are to look at.

In addition to her morning constitutional, your Pug will need to go outside about ten to fifteen minutes after each meal, immediately after waking up from a nap or engaging in spirited play, and any time she has been awake for more than

All I know is what I read in the paper.

A young Pug trying to remember whether he's supposed to be Otis or Milo.

two hours since the last time she was outside. She also ought to be taken outside the last thing before going to bed for the night and whenever she begins sniffing the floor and pacing about in a preoccupied manner. All in all, this amounts to eight trips or so a day. What's more, very young puppies cannot defer elimination for longer than roughly four hours, so you will need to take your Pug out at least once during the night until she is three or four months old.

The Pug combines a jolly disposition with a face that looks as if its owner has just been the recipient of bad news.

Do not expect your puppy to urinate and defecate every time she goes out. She ought to do one or the other on most trips, however, so do not take her back inside until you have given her ten minutes to perform. If she does draw a blank—or if your rapidly developing instinct tells you she owes you some urine or solid waste—take her back into the house, put her in her crate with a toy, and try again in about half an hour to forty-five minutes.

As your puppy matures, she will need to go outside less frequently. After she is six months old, she will be eating twice a day instead of three times, so that is one less trip, and she probably will not have to go out right after breakfast if she has gone out just before eating. Normally, our adult Pugs go out upon rising at 4:30 or 5:00 A.M., about 11:00 in the morning, 4:00 in the afternoon, and following dinner, which is served around 5:30. If they are awake for several hours before retiring, we take them out one last time.

Although our dogs are used to going out at fairly short intervals, they are capable of waiting for longer periods if necessary. In fact, we have left them alone at home on a few rare occasions for as long as ten hours without mishap.

No matter how frequently you whisk your new (or old) Pug outdoors, accidents will happen. One morning, for example, I did not notice that one of our Pugs had not defecated during her 4:30 walk. It was snowing heavily, and she was in a hurry to get back into the house for breakfast. I was preoccupied with thoughts of coffee. Not surprisingly she dirtied the kitchen floor about 8:00 A.M. I am not a great one for blaming society for an individual's crimes, but had I been paying more attention to the dog, I would have kept her outside longer, or I would have taken her outside again after breakfast.

When accidents occur, there is no point in striking a dog, pushing her face into her waste, or putting her in her crate for punishment. After all, the damage has been done already. These ill-conceived reactions do nothing to further the house-training process. Scolding or striking your dog only teaches her that you are unreliable and sometimes frightening. Stuffing her into her crate will make her associate the crate with negative feelings. These outcomes, as social scientists would say, are counterproductive. The secret of house-training—indeed, of all dog training—is to elicit the desired behavior from your dog, not to beat it into her.

Next to an observant owner, the puppy's crate is the most valuable aid in house-training. Because you have helped your puppy to learn that her crate is an inviting place, she will enter it willingly and use it as her bed during those times of the day when you cannot be with her. After she has been in her crate for any length of time, you should take her outside in case she has to eliminate.

Introducing Children

Children who are too young or immature to treat a Pug properly can pose a threat to her sense of confidence and safety. Children must be mature enough to understand that Pugs do not like to be disturbed when they are eating or sleeping, that there is a right way to hold a Pug, and that Pugs are not toys to be lugged around the house. This is why parents with toddlers should wait to buy a dog or a puppy until their children are at least four years old.

Before agreeing to sell a puppy or a dog,

breeders often want to meet a buyer's children. Conversely, buyers with children might do best to seek breeders whose puppies have been raised with youngsters underfoot.

Children do not always understand that what is fun for them may be painful for a dog. Explain that they must be careful to watch where they walk and run when the dog is around. Explain, too, that dogs often are frightened by loud, unfamiliar sounds. Ask children to speak and to play quietly until the dog gets used to them. Caution them not to pick the dog up until you feel she is comfortable enough in her new surroundings not to be traumatized by an impromptu ride. Teach children the proper way to hold a dog: one hand under her rib cage just behind the front legs, the other hand under the dog's bottom, with the dog's face pointing away from theirs. Have them practice this while sitting down in case they drop the dog or she jumps from their arms.

Dogs can inspire a sense of responsibility in children, but children never should be forced to take care of animals; and even when a child is a cooperative caregiver, parents should keep an unobtrusive eye on the dog's feeding schedule, trips outdoors, and general condition.

Introducing Other Pets

You also should be cautious when introducing a Pug to other four-legged members of the family. The chances of hostilities breaking out vary inversely with the age and tenure of the cat or dog already in residence. If you have an eight-year-old pet that always has been an only child, you probably should not get a new dog or puppy. If your pet is four years old or younger, you should be able to introduce your new Pug

if you manage the introduction carefully— and if you keep in mind how you would feel if a stranger suddenly was brought to your house for an indefinite stay without your prior approval.

If you have other pets, do not include them in the welcoming party when you bring your new Pug home. Your cat should be confined in a room, and your dog should be in her crate. After you have fraternized with your new Pug for a few hours, allow her to meet your dog. If you have more than one dog, introductions should be made one at a time.

The best way to introduce an older dog to a new one is to put the new dog in her crate before letting the old dog into the room. If the older dog sniffs at the puppy in curiosity but shows no hostility, put a lead on the older dog and let the puppy out of her crate. The less tension there is between the two dogs, the less tension you need on the lead. If your older dog flattens her ears or crouches ominously, tug on the lead with enough authority to keep her from reaching the puppy, escort her from the room, and try the introduction again the following day. If the introduction goes well, give each dog a treat, the older dog first, of course, to reinforce their civil behavior.

Before letting your cat in to see the puppy, be sure the cat's claws are clipped. As you would when introducing a dog to a puppy, place the puppy in her crate first, then let the two animals sniff at one another and exchange small talk. If your cat is lead-trained, put a lead on her when you bring her in to meet the puppy. If not, stay close to her and the puppy. Chances are, a puppy-cat introduction is not going to go as smoothly as a puppy-dog introduction, but this does not mean that your puppy and your cat will not be able to coexist peacefully.

ROUTINE CARE AND GROOMING

CHECKLIST

The Right Tools

Before you begin grooming your Pug, lay out the tools required for the task. You will need all of the following tools some of the time and some of the following tools all of the time. Your selection will be driven by the nature of the grooming session—a routine, lick-and-a-promise maintenance or a close-attention-to-details makeover:

✔ Brush(es)
✔ Cotton swabs
✔ Cotton balls
✔ Nail clippers
✔ Toothbrush and canine toothpaste
✔ Lukewarm water
✔ Vaseline
✔ Mineral oil
✔ Paper cup or other receptacle for dead hair

A pin brush with stainless steel bristles is the most usable brush for a Pug. If you want to be especially vigilant about removing dead hair, use a slicker brush or a shedding blade.

Though not as plentiful as their fawn relatives, black Pugs are equally charming and companionable.

Grooming is the art of removing dead hair from a dog so he does not have to remove it himself. Like virtue, grooming is its own reward. The more dead hair you collect from your Pug, the less you have to collect from the furniture, the rugs, your car, and your clothing.

Although a Pug's coat looks deceptively short, Pugs do shed; and their hair has a life of its own, a half life, actually, that has been reckoned at four million years. If ever there is a nuclear war, the cockroaches that inherit the earth will be wearing tiny sweaters made of Pug hair.

Ordinary dog hair, when shed, tends to lie where it falls. Not Pug hair. Just as Pugs weave their way inextricably into your life, Pug hair ingratiates itself into any fabric upon which it lands, thumbing its pushed-in nose at attempts to remove it with mere vacuum cleaners. Even the 95-horsepower vacuum tractors that one sees demonstrated on infomercials at 3:00 in the morning are unable to extract all Pug hair from your carpets and furniture.

The Pug's Grooming Schedule

Pugs should remain smart looking on a few brushings a week, and you should not have to coax them to stand still during this procedure. Being the sensual creatures that they are, Pugs thrill to the feel of a brush. When we want to groom our Pugs, all we have to do is get out the brush and sit on the floor. We are surrounded immediately by a gaggle of snorting, harrumphing customers, all declaring by their importunings that theirs is the next appointment.

Note: Pugs are equally congenial about being bathed, a subject taken up later in this chapter.

Grooming Technique

Though informal grooming parties on the floor are mutually enjoyable for you and your Pug, he should be groomed on a table once a week. Be sure to put a rubber mat or a piece of carpet with nonslip backing on the table to give him secure footing.

A well-raised Pug puppy should not be a stranger to a brush. If your new Pug is not used to being groomed, training should begin as soon as he is settled in his new surroundings. Groom him four or five minutes every two or three days until he is used to being handled.

Always brush with the lie of the coat. Do not push down constantly on the brush. Move it across your dog's body smoothly with your wrist locked. In grooming young puppies and some older dogs you will need to wield the brush with one hand while you steady the dog with the other. For example, place your free hand on the puppy's chest while you brush his back and sides; or place your free hand, palm up, on his underbelly while you brush his hindquarters or neck.

A Pug's legs are brushed or combed downward with short strokes. To groom a Pug's tail, hold it by the tip, unfurl it gently, and brush or comb gingerly with the lie of the coat.

Brushing is required not only to keep your Pug looking swell but also to allow you to look for signs of trouble in his coat. While you are brushing, check for flea dirt, skin rashes, or bald spots. If you find flea dirt, treatment with a flea-killing product is in order (see V-Flea Day, page 57). Skin rashes or bald spots merit a visit to the veterinarian, who can assess the problem and prescribe treatment.

Tough as Nails

A Pug's nails are among the fastest-growing, hardiest substances known to science. They must be clipped regularly to prevent any possibility of a Pug scratching himself, his playmates, or his two-legged friends while playing. In addition, if your Pug's nails are allowed to remain overlong, he will not stand as high on his toes as he should and may suffer a breakdown in the pasterns as a result.

A Pug's nails are among the fastest-growing substances known to humankind. They should be trimmed every other week.

Like all canines that have not become used to the idea of having their paws handled, a Pug can turn into a junkyard dog when anyone tries to clip his nails. One suspects, however, that this behavior reflects greater discredit on breeders who did not begin to clip their puppies' nails early enough than it does on their Pugs. The person from whom you acquire your Pug should have begun trimming his nails when he was two or three weeks old. If so, your Pug ought to be acclimated to the process by the time he comes to live with you. If he is not, casually hold his paws or stroke them gently for a few seconds when you are petting him or watching television together.

Nail clipping, like death and tax increases, is unavoidable. Treats and lavish praise will make the ritual more pleasant; so will a friend or family member who will hold your Pug while you clip.

Be careful to clip the hooked part of the nail only. Avoid cutting into the quick, the vein inside the nail (see illustration, page 38). Have some styptic powder handy in case you do cut into the quick and it begins to bleed. Dip a cotton swab into the styptic powder and apply it to the bleeding nail. Apologize to your Pug while the blood is coagulating and give him a treat afterward.

Ear Care

A Pug's ears are not difficult to keep clean. A few cotton swabs or cotton balls and some mineral oil or hydrogen peroxide in a small container are the only materials you need. Dip the cotton swabs or cotton balls into the oil or peroxide (the choice is yours) and swab the visible parts of the ear carefully. Do not plunge

CHECKLIST

Ears

To groom your Pug's ears properly, you will need:

✔ Cotton swabs or cotton balls

✔ Mineral oil or hydrogen peroxide

✔ Cleansing solution purchased from your veterinarian or a reputable pet store, for cleaning the lower part of the ear canal

While cleaning, remember:

✔ Never insert the cotton swab or cotton ball any farther than you can see

✔ Caked-on dirt may indicate the presence of ear mites

the cotton swab or cotton ball down into the ear canal any farther than the eye can see, or you might do some damage. If you wish to clean your Pug's lower ear canal, buy a cleaning solution from your veterinarian and follow the instructions faithfully.

If a Pug's ears exhibit caked-on dirt, he may have ear mites, the most commonly encountered ear problem in dogs and cats. The presence of mites is indicated by a dark, granular, soil-like accumulation in the ear canal. Generally, the more visible the dirt, the worse the infestation. Mites are contagious. They spread from one animal to another in situations where there is close contact among members of a clan. If you suspect that your Pug has mites, schedule an appointment with a veterinarian.

Pugs are a wash-and-wear, drip-dry, fashionably wrinkled breed.

'Tis better to remove dead hair from the Pug than it is from the rug.

Wrinkle-free Wrinkles

A Pug's facial wrinkles, which contribute to his singular appearance, may also contribute to his discomfort—and to a certain clam-bog odor about him—if they are not cleaned regularly. Wrinkles mimic the space between the cushions and the back of the couch by forming a repository for excess food, tears, or other discharges from the eyes. Wrinkles must, therefore, be kept clean.

Once a week, or sooner if your Pug's face begins smelling boggy, hold your Pug's head gently in one hand and, with a cotton swab that has been dipped in warm water, clean any dirt or caked tears from your Pug's nose wrinkle. Be sure to wield the cotton swab delicately. Pugs are proud of their faces, and they are generally disinclined to having you mucking about in their nose wrinkles.

Clean the smaller wrinkles under your Pug's eyes in the same manner, and after you have mined his wrinkles, spread a thin application of Vaseline in them with a cotton swab. If you notice bald spots or a rash in your Pug's wrinkles, take him to the veterinarian to determine whether he (your Pug) is growing a fungus.

Bathing Your Pug

Some people bathe their Pugs in the kitchen sink. We find it more comfortable to bathe ours, once they are full-grown, in the bathtub. Whichever you prefer, a spray attachment is an indispensably helpful option.

Before placing your Pug in the tub, lay out the implements you will need for the bathing ceremony. These include:
✔ Brush(es)
✔ Shampoo
✔ Two or three bath towels
✔ Cotton balls
✔ Cotton swabs
✔ Mineral oil in a squeeze bottle
✔ Hair dryer (optional)

1. Clean your Pug's ears if necessary (see page 39) before putting him into the tub, and put a small wad of cotton into each ear to prevent water from reaching the ear canal and possibly causing infection.

2. Put a few drops of eye ointment into each of his eyes to protect them from stray

Like the crevices between sofa cushions and the back of the sofa, a Pug's wrinkles are a repository for debris. A weekly cleaning with a Q-tip will help to keep the wrinkles free of infection.

Wet your Pug thoroughly with lukewarm water before applying the shampoo.

shampoo. If his face needs washing, attend to that, too, before you bathe him.

3. Put a rubber mat or a bath towel in the bottom of the tub to provide secure footing for your Pug.

4. Turn on the water and adjust the temperature, testing it with your wrist. If the water feels uncomfortably warm to you, chances are it will to your Pug. Adjust accordingly until the water is comfortably lukewarm. Make sure, too, that the house temperature is at least 72°F (22°C).

5. Wet your Pug thoroughly after putting him in the tub, making sure the water penetrates to his skin, then apply the shampoo, lathering the coat generously. Never lather past your Pug's neck or you risk getting shampoo into his eyes. Allow the shampoo to remain in his coat for whatever length of time the manufacturer recommends before rinsing.

After your Pug has been lathered and rinsed—you are finished rinsing when the water coming off him is as clean as the water going onto him—remove him from the sink and wrap him in a towel. Use another towel to dry him more thoroughly.

Because baths are stimulating for our Pugs, we take them outside for a quick run after toweling them dry. Watching them race around in the low-rider crouch, which has to be seen to be appreciated, more than makes up for having to clean the mess in the bathroom and the necessity of changing one's wet clothes.

FOOD FOR THOUGHT

Dog food is not hard to find. Supermarkets, convenience stores, pet shops, feed-and-seed emporiums, discount-buying clubs, and veterinarians will gladly sell you all you need, and some of those places will even have an employee carry it out to the car for you. The tricky part, and it really isn't all that tricky, is sorting your way through the boxes, bags, cans, and manufacturers' claims about stronger bones, healthier teeth, and superior moral fiber.

Fortunately, you don't have to take a home-study course in animal nutrition in order to feed your dog properly. In fact, you don't have to know a dispensable amino acid from an indispensable one—or the number of amino acids a dog requires—to be a good provider. All you need are a few coping strategies and some common sense. The former, of course, you can acquire by reading this chapter.

Dry, Semimoist, or Canned?

Dog food is available in three configurations—dry, moist, and semimoist. Dry food is less expensive, easier to store, and more convenient to use than moist, also known as canned, food. Dry food also helps to reduce dental plaque to some extent. Canned food is gener-

In Pugs as in yo-yos, walking the dog requires a calm, steady hand and occasional practice.

ally more tasty and, because it is 75 percent moisture, is a better source of water than other foods. (Dry food contains roughly 10 percent water; semimoist contains 33 percent.)

Dry food is the dog owner's favorite. It sold to the tune of $3.1 billion in 1996, accounting for 71 percent of total dog food expenditures, according to the Maxwell Report, a comprehensive study of the pet food industry. Canned food was second in popularity, accounting for 28 percent of dog food sales. Semimoist food, because of its high chemical content—preservatives and coloring agents—and its relatively higher price, occupied a much smaller sliver of the dog-food pie, barely 1 percent.

Making Sense of Dog Food Labels

Reading a dog food label is like squinting at the last line on an eye examination chart. You cannot be certain if you're seeing what you think you're seeing, and even when you are certain, you're reading only letters, not words, letters such as *m-e-n-a-d-i-o-n-e s-o-d-i-u-m b-i-s-u-l-f-i-t-e*. Fortunately, the most significant passage on a dog food label, the nutritional claim made by the manufacturer, is written in plain English.

Nutritional claims come in two varieties. In the first the manufacturer declares that "Bowser Bits" has been shown to provide complete and balanced nutrition in feeding trials conducted according to the Association of American Feed Control Officials (AAFCO) protocols. In the second kind of nutritional claim the manufacturer attests that "Bowser Bits" has been formulated to meet the various levels established in AAFCO's nutrient profiles.

In order to make the feeding-trials claim a manufacturer must compare data obtained from an experimental and a control group of dogs, each of which must contain at least eight members. The dogs in the experimental group are fed only "Bowser Bits" for a specified period of time, while the control group is fed a diet already known to be complete and balanced. At the end of the test period, if the dogs fed "Bowser Bits" do not differ significantly along certain variables from the control group, the manufacturer is entitled to claim that "Bowser Bits" provides complete and balanced nutrition according to AAFCO's feed-trial protocols. The variables on which the experimental and control groups are compared include weight, skin and coat condition, red-blood-cell count, and other health measures.

In order to make the second kind of nutritional claim—that "Bowser Bits" was formulated to meet the levels established in AAFCO nutrient profiles—manufacturers must sign an affidavit stating that "Bowser Bits" was formulated from ingredients that will contain, after they have been processed, sufficient levels of all the nutrients AAFCO has determined a dog food should contain.

The difference between buying a dog food that has been tested in feed trials and one that has been formulated to meet AAFCO profiles is like the difference between buying a preferred stock and a futures option: The consumer can be more confident that the preferred stock—the feed-tested dog food—is going to perform the way it is supposed to perform because it has been fed to real dogs in real feeding trials.

The meets-the-nutrient-profiles statement, on the other hand, is somewhat misleading. It does not mean that AAFCO has analyzed the food in question and has certified that it meets organization standards. Nor does the statement necessarily mean that the manufacturer tested the food to determine whether it met AAFCO profiles. This statement simply means the manufacturer formulated the food from ingredients that should have provided enough nutrients to meet the AAFCO profile. We say "should have" because cooking always destroys nutrients in dog food to some extent. Therefore, the nutrients that go into the kettle are always present in greater amounts than the nutrients that go into the can.

Thus far we have discussed only one part of the nutritional claim made on dog food labels—the part that tells you the basis on which manufacturers state their claims. There is, however, a second part to nutritional statements: the part that specifies the dogs for which the food is intended. Thus, a complete nutritional claim for a feed-tested food will say: "Animal feeding tests using AAFCO procedures substantiate that 'Bowser Bits' provides complete and balanced nutrition for all life stages of the dog." A complete nutritional claim for a meets-the-profile food will say: "'Bowser Bits' is formulated to meet the nutrient levels established by AAFCO nutrient profiles for all stages of a dog's life." Both these statements assure consumers that they can feed an all-life-stages food to their dogs from puppyhood through seniorhood, including motherhood, without worrying.

Instead of being formulated for all stages of a dog's life, some foods are intended for the maintenance of adult dogs only, and other foods are intended to support growth and reproduction. The latter, formulated to meet the increased nutritional needs of pregnant females and puppies, must contain more of certain nutrients—more protein, calcium, phosphorus, sodium, and chloride, for example—than do maintenance foods. Foods providing complete and balanced nutrition for all life stages of a dog also must meet growth and reproduction standards.

In addition, several companies produce senior-citizen foods for older dogs. These foods, which must satisfy maintenance requirements in order to make the complete-and-balanced claim, are based on two principles: Older dogs need less of certain nutrients—proteins, phosphorus, and salt, for example—than do younger dogs, and older dogs are less able to tolerate nutrient excess than younger dogs are.

Special Diets

Dogs are put on special diets for several reasons—illness, old age, or obesity among them. Dogs with hypertension, heart disease, or edema (swelling) should be on low-sodium diets. Dogs with kidney or liver conditions should be fed diets low in protein, phosphorus, and sodium. Dogs that are underweight or that suffer from pancreatic or liver disease should be fed highly digestible food. If any of these or other conditions are diagnosed by a veterinarian, he or she may recommend a special diet. You should follow the veterinarian's instructions faithfully, and, of course, never feed a special diet to a Pug without first consulting a veterinarian.

Other special foods have been formulated to sculpt the overweight dog into a fit-and-trim specimen. Diet dog food, usually called "lite," allows you to feed the same amount of food while lowering a dog's caloric intake. Lite food contains 20 to 33 percent fewer calories than regular food does. Like other special diets, lite food should be fed only to those dogs for whom veterinarians recommend it.

Snacks and Treats

There is no more jolly and attentive audience than Pug dogs contemplating a treat. Their nostrils flare, their bodies quiver from head to tail, their breath comes in fiery snorts, and their eyes threaten to pop out of their precious little heads.

TIP

More Isn't Better

If a commercial dog food is labeled nutritionally complete and balanced, there is no reason to add vitamin or mineral supplements to it. Additional vitamins may upset the balance of vitamins already in the food and may cause vitamin toxicity. The only dogs needing vitamin or mineral supplements are those not eating properly because of illness or those losing increased amounts of body fluids because of diarrhea or increased urination. Dogs in either of those categories should be seen by a veterinarian, who may recommend a vitamin or mineral supplement.

Chewies du jour are always popular appetizers on any Pug's menu.

A considerable subset of the pet food industry is built on this response. Indeed, 20 cents of every dollar spent on dog food is spent on snacks, but dog owners should remember that snacks and treats are nutritionally deficient for full-time use. Moreover, a dog is going to want them full-time if you offer them too frequently.

In deciding how many treats and snacks to give your dog, let the label be your guide. If the label says, "'Bowser Beef Wellington Bits' are intended for intermittent or supplemental use only," then use them intermittently. Do not allow snacks and treats to comprise more than 5 to 10 percent of your dog's diet.

Chew Toys

No entrepreneur ever went broke overestimating the dog's fondness for chewing. Upon meeting a strange object, a dog generally exer-

cises one of two options: If it moves, the dog barks at it. If it stands still, the dog gnaws on it. (Male dogs, of course, may exercise a third option.) That is why supermarkets, pet shops, and feed stores bristle with an *al dente* selection of chewables.

Chew toys are based on the principle that a dog's teeth are certified erogenous zones. If you want to send a dog into terminal euphoria, bring home a sweaty, smoked-and-processed pig's ear, set it on the floor, and announce, "Let the gnawing begin." Several hours later your dog will have achieved a state of bliss known only to mystics, Phish fans, and lottery winners.

Chewables, like any other source of pleasure, can also be a source of pain. Chicken bones should be avoided entirely because they can splinter, get lodged in a dog's throat, or poke holes in her stomach or intestines. Many Pug owners who give their dogs marrow or knuckle bones recommend roasting them in a 175°F (79°C) oven for twenty minutes to kill any harmful bacteria.

Processed cowhide, generally known as rawhide, is the astroturf of the bone world. Long aware of the dog's fondness for chewing, pet supply manufacturers routinely paint, process, and press rawhide into "bones" for your dog's chewing enjoyment. Some rawhide bones are a bleached-looking white, others an off-cream, and still others, which have been basted, broasted, broiled, or roasted, come in colors for which there are no words. In addition to being basted or broasted, some bones are chicken, beef, hickory, cheese, peanut butter, or, for those Pugs expecting company, mint flavored. Because of its flexibility, rawhide also can be fashioned into surreal approximations of tacos, lollipops, cocktail franks, bagels, french fries, and giant pretzels to appeal to human tastes.

A Pug could come to grief by chewing off pieces of rawhide and swallowing them, so be sure to monitor your Pug carefully the first few times you present her with a rawhide chew toy. If she shows an inclination to chew off pieces of the toy, give her something more substantial to chew on instead, such as a bone made of hard nylon.

Given manufacturers' ingenuity, one suspects that soon it will be possible to give a dog a different chewable treat every day of the year without giving a treat of the same size, shape, color, and flavor more than once. Yet whether

Pugs work diligently to maintain their velour-covered-sausage physiques.

your Pug prefers rawhide watermelon slices or marrow bones tartare, all chewables should be served inside the house. A Pug gnawing happily on a chewy treat in the backyard soon will be attended by a retinue of ants, flies, bees, if they are in season, and other uninvited vermin.

How Much and How Often to Feed

The amount of food a dog requires is determined by his or her age, condition, metabolism, environment, biological status, activity level, and ability to convert food into energy and heat. Variations in the effect of these factors among Pugs can make generalizations, not to

mention feeding charts, something of a Pug in a poke.

If there is one generalization to be made regarding weight, it is this: The amounts specified in feeding charts on dog food packages and cans are far too generous. Like the manufacturers of soap powder and shampoo, the makers of dog food usually overestimate the amount of their product a person needs to use in order to produce the desired results. The generosity on the part of dog food manufacturers is understandable. They would be embarrassed if dogs were to lose weight on the recommended amounts. Therefore, they recommend high.

During their first year, Pugs' food requirements diminish somewhat. From the age of three months, about the earliest that a Pug should be going to its new home, until six months of age, Pugs should eat three times a day. Each meal should consist, roughly, of $\frac{1}{3}$ cup (79 ml) of dry puppy chow, marinated briefly in warm tap water, and 1 or 2 tablespoons (15 ml) of canned all-life-stages food.

Our Pugs would happily observe this schedule the rest of their merry lives, but we switch them to two meals a day when they're six months old. Each of those meals comprises, roughly, $\frac{1}{2}$ cup (118 ml) of dry puppy chow, marinated briefly in warm tap water, and 1 or 2 tablespoons (15 ml) of canned all-life-stages food.

When our Pugs celebrate their first birthdays, we switch them to $\frac{1}{2}$ cup (118 ml) of water-marinated dry food designed to accommodate all life stages of a dog and 1 or 2 tablespoons (15 ml) of canned, all-life-stages food. As Pugs get older, they tend to become more sedentary and, thus, to gain weight. All of our older Pugs—that is, those more than four years old—get $\frac{1}{3}$ cup (79 ml) of "lite" dry food, marinated briefly in warm tap water, and 1 or 2 tablespoons (15 ml) of canned food.

What Should a Pug Weigh?

It is difficult to venture what any Pug should weigh without knowing something about her bone structure, muscle development, and height. According to the American Kennel Club breed standard for Pugs, it is "desirable" that they should weigh between 14 and 18 pounds (6.3 to 8.2 kg), but this is not a reliable guide to any single dog's ideal weight. A large-boned male 13 inches (33 cm) at the withers would be dolefully underweight at 14 pounds (6.3 kg). A fine-boned female 10 inches (25 cm) at the withers would be close to obese at 18 pounds (8.2 kg).

Instead of looking only at the scale to determine if your Pug exceeds or falls short of her desirable weight, look closely at her as well. If you can see her ribs, she's too skinny. If you run your hand gently down her back from shoulders to tail and you feel the spinous processes that stick out along the spine, or if during the same inspection you can feel the transverse processes that protrude sideways from the spine, your Pug is too thin.

If your Pug has an hour-glass figure or if you cannot feel her ribs readily, she is too fat. Additional bouquets of fat are likely to blossom on the brisket (the area below the chest and between the forelegs), the neck, the abdomen, and the point at which the tail meets the body. If any of these spots seems too well padded, perhaps your Pug is too well fed. If you cannot see your dog's ribs but you can feel them without having to squeeze her sides, she is probably neither too fat nor too thin.

Burdens of Excess Weight

Whether you acquire a twelve-week-old flurry of feet and kisses or a mature adult, there is a direct and incontrovertible relationship between what you put into your Pug's bowl and the quantity of muscle and fat she develops. There also is a relationship between her weight and her state of health. Although excess weight is wrongly indicted for causing everything from heart problems to dislocated kneecaps, there is no denying that too much weight is often a contributing factor—and is almost always a complicating one—in many health-compromising conditions.

In addition to aggravating locomotor problems, excess weight will aggravate a collapsing trachea, an inherited condition common in toy breeds, in which the rings of cartilage in the windpipe collapse. Excess weight also makes it more difficult for Pugs to dissipate heat in sultry weather, a problem already common to all members of the breed, fat or thin. Moreover, dogs, like people, are subject to an increasing litany of troubles as they grow older, and Pugs that are overweight when the specter of old age comes calling are saddled with an unfair handicap in fighting disease and infirmity. It is difficult to specify the point at which a Pug's health could be compromised by surplus weight, but most females in excess of 19 pounds (8.6 kg) and most males in excess of 23 pounds (10.4 kg) are candidates for less food and more exercise.

TIP

Switching Diets

When you get your Pug, find out what kind of food she is used to eating. If that diet, whether commercial or homemade, is both sound for the puppy and convenient for you to feed, continue feeding it.

If you want to switch foods—which you probably will if you buy a puppy that has been raised on a homemade diet and you would prefer to leave the measuring and stirring to the pet food companies—fold a suitable new food into the puppy's previous food in a one-part-new-to-three-parts-old ratio. Every three or four days increase the new food while decreasing the old until the changeover is complete.

THE HEALTHY PUG

As we noted in The Puppy Checklist (page 19), Pug dogs tell us how they're feeling by the way they look and behave. When they're feeling well:
✔ Their eyes are bright and gleaming.
✔ Their noses are cool and slightly damp.
✔ Their gums are neither pale nor inflamed.
✔ Their ears are free of dirt and wax.
✔ Their bodies are fit and well muscled, a little padded, perhaps, but not paunchy and never seriously thin.
✔ Their coats are plush and immaculate without bald patches, scabs, or flea dirt.
✔ The area below their tails is unmarred by inflammation, dried waste, lumpy growths, or discoloration.

Although they spend prodigious amounts of time in sleep—a good fourteen to sixteen hours a day—Pugs are otherwise active and alert. They display affection for their owners, a zest for adventure, a fearless approach to life, and a keen interest in mealtimes.

If Symptoms Persist

Frequently the first suggestion that a Pug is unwell is a lack of interest in food. One missed meal or a faint, desultory pass at the plate is cause for some apprehension; and the Pug that misses two consecutive meals merits a call to the veterinarian, who probably will want to

A fetching youg Pug enjoying a Hallmark moment.

know if that Pug's temperature is elevated or if he displays additional symptoms of potential illness such as vomiting or diarrhea.

Do not worry about making a pest of yourself by calling your veterinarian whenever your Pug does not seem right. No caring veterinarian will be annoyed by hearing from a caring owner, no matter how slight the symptom(s) the owner has called to report. Nor should you hesitate to seek another opinion if you have any reservations about the way your veterinarian is treating your Pug.

When our Pug Debbie was fifteen months old, she woke up sneezing about 3:00 one Saturday morning. Because her nose was a little runny, too, we had her to the veterinarian's office by 9:30 A.M. Her lungs sounded normal, her temperature wasn't elevated, and she had eaten breakfast. Thus, the veterinarian concluded that Debbie might be growing an upper respiratory infection. We left the office with some antibiotics and instructions to call back on Monday if Debbie was not well.

During the weekend Debbie became more lethargic and less interested in eating. When the veterinarian reexamined her on Monday, Debbie's lungs were taking on fluid, her temperature was elevated, and the diagnosis was pneumonia. We left the office with stronger antibiotics, a diuretic, and instructions to call again if Debbie was not well by Thursday.

I feared that Debbie was not going to be around by Thursday at the rate she was going. When she would not eat at all Monday night

CHECKLIST

Signs of Illness

Lack of interest in food is not the only, or always the first, sign of illness. You should call your veterinarian if the answer is yes to any of the following questions:

✔ Is your Pug's breathing labored?

✔ Has he been coughing, gagging, or sneezing?

✔ Is he drinking more water than usual?

✔ Has he been favoring one leg when he walks?

✔ Is he dragging his hindquarters across the floor?

✔ Does he have a swelling or an abscess on his body?

✔ Is he scratching, licking, or chewing himself excessively?

✔ Is there an immoderate amount of flea dirt in his coat?

✔ Are his eyes runny, cloudy, or bloodshot?

✔ Have you noticed worms in his stools?

✔ Is there blood in his urine or stools?

✔ Has he been shaking his head frequently?

✔ Has he been lethargic for any length of time?

✔ Has he been digging at his ears?

✔ Are his gums inflamed?

✔ Is his nose runny?

✔ Is his breath foul?

or Tuesday morning, I called another veterinarian and was in his office with Debbie by 7:30 that night. After examining the dog, he informed my wife and me that Debbie would not be going home with us. He planned to quadruple her diuretic and to put her on intravenous antibiotics and fluids. He was also going to do a cardiogram and consult by phone with specialists in New York.

We called the veterinarian twice on Wednesday. The second time he told us that Debbie had begun to eat. I asked if we might visit her on Thursday. He said that was all right.

We arrived on Thursday with our other Pug and half a pound of white meat turkey from the delicatessen. When Debbie fell on the turkey and then tried to assume the dominance position by putting her front legs on our other Pug's shoulders, we fairly broke into cheers.

Debbie was released the next day. She had to go back to the veterinarian's for X-rays twice during the following weeks to make sure the fluid had receded from her lungs. I am convinced the second veterinarian saved her life. I hope you are convinced that one of your many functions as a Pug owner is that of medical advocate.

Vaccinations

Until they are roughly six to eight weeks old, puppies are protected from certain diseases by antibodies in their mothers' milk, as long as their mothers have been immunized properly against those diseases and possess sufficient antibodies to confer immunity. Because this passive immunity interferes with puppies' ability to produce antibodies in response to vaccinations, they are not vaccinated for the first time until they are at least six weeks old.

The vaccines given to puppies and dogs contain antigens that have been derived ultimately from viruses or bacteria obtained from live animals. At the appropriate intervals—usually at eight, twelve, and sixteen weeks of age—a puppy should be vaccinated against the following diseases:

✔ Distemper—an airborne viral disease that affects the lungs, intestines, and brain.
✔ Hepatitis—a viral disease of the liver.
✔ Leptospirosis—a bacterial disease that attacks the urinary system.
✔ Parainfluenza—infectious bronchitis.
✔ Parvovirus—a viral disease of the intestines.
✔ Corona viruses, which attack the intestines.

Booster shots that protect against these diseases are administered when a dog is fourteen months old and every twelve months thereafter. Rabies vaccinations are administered at six months, eighteen months, and every three years thereafter.

✔ In addition, dogs that are kept in close quarters with numerous other dogs may be vaccinated against *bordetella,* also known as kennel cough. This vaccine is further indicated for dogs being boarded in kennels and those involved in commercial and/or international travel.

✔ Finally, Lyme disease vaccine is recommended for dogs living in or spending any time in areas where this tick-borne disease is a health threat.

When the antigens representing the above-mentioned diseases begin circulating in the puppy's bloodstream, they are detected and seized upon by specialized cells that are part of the body's immune system. After a series of complex evolutions, the puppy's immune system produces cells that are able to detect and destroy the diseases represented by the antigens in a vaccine. Thus, if a dog vaccinated against distemper is later exposed to the virus, distemper antibodies will recognize and exterminate any free-ranging distemper virus particles at large in the bloodstream. And if the distemper invaders manage to infect some of the dog's cells, those infected cells will be recognized, destroyed, and shown the door by other specialized cells in the immune system.

Importance of Booster Shots

One vaccination, however, does not confer instant immunity on a puppy. Not for five to ten days will a puppy's immune system start to forge a response to the challenge posed by the antigens in a vaccine. That response is low grade and not entirely effective. What's more, one can never be certain how long a puppy's passive immunity will continue to compromise his ability to manufacture his own antibodies. This is why veterinarians administer two additional vaccine series at three- to four-week intervals. After that, dogs should receive booster shots once a year because antibodies decrease in number over time and the immune system needs to be stimulated to produce additional disease-fighting troops.

External Parasites

Parasites are living organisms that reside in or on other living organisms, called hosts, feeding on blood, lymph cells, or tissue. Internal parasites dwell inside their hosts. External parasites live on the surface of their hosts.

The external parasites to which a dog is the unwitting landlord include fleas, ticks, flies, lice, larvae, and mites. This motley collection of

insects and arachnids, in addition to damaging skin tissue, may transmit harmful bacteria and menacing viruses to your Pug. In significant quantities external parasites can sap your Pug's energy, weaken his resistance to infection and disease, and bequeath to him a number of diseases and/or parasitic worms.

The presence of external parasites is usually revealed by flea dirt, skin lesions, pustules, hair loss, itching, redness, dandruff, scaling, scabs, growths of thickened skin, or an unpleasant odor. If your Pug begins to scratch or bite at himself excessively, or if you notice any of these symptoms while you are grooming him, call your veterinarian. She or he will prescribe a course of treatment. The earlier that external parasites are detected, the easier they are to banish. This, among other reasons, is why you should groom your Pug regularly.

"The other vet always forgets to put the flap down when he's finished."

Humans, too, can be affected by some of the external parasites troubling their dogs. If flea infestation is severe enough, fleas may dine on humans temporarily. Certain kinds of mites will migrate to humans, and so will ticks. Especially worrisome to humans are ticks that carry Rocky Mountain spotted fever and Lyme disease. The latter is the most common tick-borne disease in the United States.

Pugs afflicted with external parasites will have to be treated with parasiticidal dips, powders, ointments, and/or shampoos. Always follow your veterinarian's instructions when using these products.

Fleas: The Bad Old Days

Eternal vigilance was once the price of a flealess Pug. The daily flea comb and the biweekly flea bath were the most prominent engagements on the Pug owner's social calendar during flea season, which seemed to grow longer with each passing year. Owners resorted to an ever-expanding battery of potions, lotions, shampoos, sprays, powders, mousses, bombs, roll-ons, flea collars, dips, herbs, electronic transmitters, spells, and other talismans designed to kill fleas.

Thus it was and thus it ever had been. If you had a dog, your dog had fleas. They went with the territory. Sometimes the flea population seemed so entrenched that I began to believe our fleas had fleas. If that strikes you as a paranoid delusion brought on by excessive exposure to the chemicals in flea-fighting products, consider the following from Jonathan Swift (1667–1745): "So, naturalists observe, a flea/Hath smaller fleas that on him prey;/And these have smaller fleas that bite 'em;/And so proceed ad infinitum."

Short of moving to an arctic or a mile-high climate, there was little a Pug owner could do about fleas but comb and spray, and bathe and comb, and spray and bomb, hoping for deliverance while cursing the fates.

V-Flea Day

Sometimes in this troublesome world it isn't always darkest just before the lights go out. If you don't believe me, consider the following pronouncement that appeared in *Newsday* on October 5, 1996: "Mankind has won the flea wars . . . . It's over. No more dips. No more bombs. No more vacuuming the draperies. The 70 million pet owners who comprise our side are still standing. The losses on the other side were so great, V-Flea Day was recently declared."

The writer's attack of euphoria was brought on by the battlefield successes of Program, Advantage, and Frontline against the legions of the flea. Program, which was introduced in 1995, is a once-a-month tablet that turns your dog into a mobile spay clinic. When a female flea bites a dog whose owner has gotten with the Program, lufenuron, the operative ingredient in Program, prevents the flea's eggs and larvae from developing into adult fleas, and reproducing.

Although Program doesn't kill fleas, it can bring a code red flea infestation under control within thirty to ninety days—quicker if it's combined with traditional flea-treating methods such as vacuuming and bathing. A grateful pet-owning public made Program, which is sold only

"One-oh-three-point-five. That's not so good is it?"

by veterinarians, the all-time best-selling veterinary product in its first year on the market.

The following year two new flea-killing products were introduced: Advantage and Frontline. These topical solutions, which are also sold only by veterinarians, are packaged in squeeze tubes and are applied to the area between a dog's shoulder blades. Hence they are known as spot-ons. They spread from the shoulder throughout the surface of the skin, but do not enter the bloodstream. They kill fleas on contact, so even if a flea lands on your Pug and decides not to stay for dinner, within two hours it's lights out for the hopper.

The active ingredients in these marvels, which are gentle enough to use on dogs, puppies, cats, and kittens, collect in the hair follicles and oil-producing glands of the skin. There they remain protected against removal by shampooing, swimming, or sudden rainstorms. Both Advantage and Frontline continually reapply themselves to your pet's hair, providing long-lasting, effective flea control. Frontline, which is available in a spray

form as well as a spot-on, also kills ticks, including the varmints that carry human and canine Lyme disease, Rocky Mountain spotted fever, erlichiosis, and babesiosis.

The commercial success of Advantage and Frontline inspired the introduction of similar spot-on products—Bio-Spot, Ovi-Spot Plus, Zodiac Powerspot, and Hartz OneSpot—that can be purchased through pet-supply warehouses and at pet stores. Bio-Spot kills flea eggs, larvae, adult fleas, ticks, and mosquitoes, which have been indicted as heartworm carriers. Ovi-Spot Plus is effective against fleas and ticks, and it prevents flea eggs from hatching. Zodiac Powerspot kills adult fleas, flea eggs, larvae, and ticks. Hartz OneSpot kills fleas, flea eggs, and ticks.

The writer who declared victory in the war against fleas wasn't just whistling "The Halls of Montezuma." These products work, and they're bulletproof. We have used several of them, and since we have, we haven't seen fleas on or about our dogs or cats. The results are nigh on to miraculous. These products have our vote for the most beneficial improvements introduced during the twentieth century. We'd sooner do without cell phones, call waiting, aroma therapy, instant messaging, and a lot of the other, more highly touted advances than we would these awesome products. Indeed, such is their efficiency that we needn't bother to discuss collars, dips, shampoos, or any of the relics of the bad old days. Why go to battle with a single-shot rifle when you've got the equivalent of the neutron bomb at your disposal?

Internal Parasites

Protozoa and worms are the internal parasites to which a dog is host. Protozoa are usually one-celled organisms that may contain specialized structures for feeding and locomotion. One protozoan sometimes found in dogs is *Toxoplasma gondii*, which is carried in oocysts shed in cat feces. If you have a cat, do not allow your Pug to go truffle hunting in the litterbox. Fortunately, the threat of your Pug's being infected by *T. gondii* from your cat is limited. Once a cat's immune system responds to *T. gondii*, the cat stops shedding oocysts.

Note: Coccidia, another protozoan disease, is usually found in young dogs kept in crowded conditions.

The presence of three kinds of worms that infest dogs—roundworms, hookworms, and whipworms—can be detected through stool sample analysis. Tapeworms, however, are not amenable to this method of identification. They are best identified by the time-honored technique of lifting a dog's tail and peering studiously at his anus. During this examination, the inspector is looking for small, white tapeworm segments that look like reborn stir-fried rice. These segments also can be seen on freshly minted stools.

The presence of heartworms can be detected by blood-sample analysis. If your Pug is negative for heartworms, your veterinarian can prescribe preventive heartworm medication to keep him that way. If your Pug tests positive for heartworms, he will require treatment that may include hospitalization and/or surgery.

Most worms, despite their repugnance, are not difficult to control. When you acquire a Pug, ask the person from whom you get him when he (the Pug) was last dewormed and what deworming agent he was given. To be safe, take a stool sample and your new Pug's previous deworming history to your veterinarian, who will recommend a safe, effective deworming agent and will set up a deworming schedule.

Keeping the Pearly Gates Pearly

Clean teeth, in addition to being things of beauty and a joy, one hopes, forever, may help to prevent certain diseases of the heart, liver, and kidneys that are thought to be caused by the spread of bacteria from a dog's mouth. Diligent Pug owners, therefore, do not allow poor dental hygiene to put the bite on their dogs' health.

Dry dog foods, which ought to comprise the bulk of a Pug's diet, help to a certain extent to reduce plaque—the sticky combination of bacteria, food particles, and saliva that is constantly forming and hardening on the teeth. Unfortunately, dry foods are not an unalloyed dental blessing. The carbohydrates in dry foods stick to the teeth and act as compost for the bacteria that is plaque's main ingredient.

Note: Canned dog foods do nothing to remove plaque. What's more, the sugar they contain adds to its buildup.

Pugs are willing to assist in their own dental care by chewing on rawhide bones, knuckle bones, marrowbones, or bones made of hard nylon. Encourage this participation by allowing your Pug to floss with some kind of bone or specially designed teeth-cleaning toy once or twice a week.

If plaque is not removed regularly from your Pug's teeth—by you or by your Pug—it hardens into calculus (tartar) and intrudes itself

Brushing your Pug's teeth regularly will help to prevent poor dental hygiene from putting the bite on her health.

between the teeth and gums, creating a tiny sinkhole in which bacteria multiply. These bacteria invade the gingiva (gum), causing it to become inflamed, to swell, and to bleed when probed. This condition, known as gingivitis, is reversible if treated early in its development. If not, it escalates into periodontitis, ulceration of the gums and erosion of the alveolar bone, which holds the teeth in place. Periodontitis is not reversible, and if it is not controlled, the gums and alveolar bone eventually become so eroded that the teeth fall out.

To check for signs of gingivitis, gently but firmly hold your Pug's head with one hand and lift his upper lip along one side of his mouth with the other hand. Look closely at his teeth and gums. Repeat this procedure on the opposite side and in the front of his mouth, then inspect his bottom teeth in the same fashion. If there is a red line along his gums, make an appointment to have your veterinarian check your Pug's teeth.

Other signs of oral disease include perpetual morning breath, avoidance of dry food, resistance to being stroked on the muzzle, brown or yellow crust on tooth surfaces, loss of appetite, and drooling. If your dog exhibits

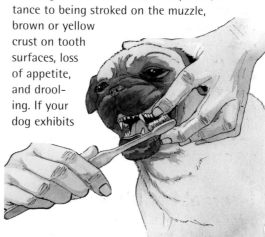

any of these symptoms, call your veterinarian and describe the dog's behavior.

You can assist your Pug in keeping his teeth clean by brushing them once or twice a week. Introduce this idea gradually by playing a game of "See the Doggie's Teeth" each day. Look at his teeth as you did during the gingivitis inspection, but in addition to just looking, rub a finger along his teeth, first in front of them and then behind them.

When your Pug is used to this game, substitute a soft-bristle, child's toothbrush or a finger brush made especially for dogs in place of your own finger. You will want to add canine toothpaste to whatever brush you choose. Your veterinarian will be able to recommend a suitable one.

The Pug believes, quite sensibly, that a little exercise goes a long way.

Warning: Never use human toothpaste on your dog's teeth. The foaming agent it contains can cause gastric problems in dogs. Also avoid using baking soda or salt to clean your dog's teeth. These substances do not remove plaque effectively, and they contain sodium, which can be harmful to older dogs with heart disease.

Medicating and Feeding a Sick Pug

Ignorance is bliss when medicating a Pug. As long as the Pug remains ignorant of the

contents of the mound of baby food you offer on a tablespoon or on the tips of your fingers, the pill hidden in that mound of food should go down blissfully. If your Pug is too sick to eat, pills may have to be administered manually or with a pill gun. The latter is available in a pet shop, a pet supply catalog, or an Internet site. In any event the technique is the same: Place the pill as far back on your Pug's tongue as possible, hold his mouth shut, and stroke his throat until he swallows. Do not forget to praise him when he does.

Pugs convalescing from an illness or injury must consume enough fluid to replace what they lose through elimination and panting. If your Pug is unwilling to drink, you will have to

Pugs willingly take their medicine when it's disguised as a snack.

get nourishing liquids—water or broths—down his throat one way or another.

Spooning fluid into a Pug's mouth can be messy and uncomfortable for you and for him. A syringe or a spray bottle is a better choice. Your veterinarian can tell you how much fluid your Pug should receive daily.

If your Pug is off his feed, switch to an all-canned-food diet and warm the food slightly in the microwave to release its aromas before giving it to him. Be sure to stir the warmed food and to test it for pockets of heat before offering it to your Pug.

When a Pug is not eating, virtually any food is nutritious food for the time being. Baby food, turkey or chicken from the deli, canned dog food marinated in beef or chicken broth, hamburger seasoned with garlic, broth straight up, anything that will revive your Pug's interest in eating. In serious cases you may have to feed your Pug a pureed diet with a large syringe.

Exercise

Pugs, being the civilized creatures they are, do not require much exercise. They like being outdoors, though, and if at all possible, should be provided with a securely fenced yard in which they can race about when the spirit moves them. They need not spend long amounts of time in the yard. An hour or so in the morning and again in the afternoon, weather permitting—and with access to fresh water, of course—is sufficient. Pugs that live in houses or apartments without yards should be walked fifteen or twenty minutes at least once a day, in addition to their constitutional walks, and should be taken two or three times a week to an area where they can enjoy a good run under their owners' supervision.

Gifts often come with strings attached, and the Pug's modest exercise needs are a case in point. Hot or humid weather is a challenge to a Pug's respiration system, which has been compromised rather severely for the sake of a short nose. Pug owners, therefore, should have an accurate outdoor thermometer mounted somewhere near the yard. When the temperature reaches 85°F (29.4°C), do not leave your Pug outdoors for more than ten or fifteen minutes. To do otherwise is to court heatstroke (see HOW-TO: Emergencies, page 66).

Inherited Problems in Pugs

Like all pedigreed dogs, Pugs are subject to a number of inherited disease conditions. The following are the ones most frequently encountered:

Legg-Perthes is a degeneration of the head of the femur bone, the long upper bone of the hind leg. It usually occurs before a Pug is ten months old. Anyone who acquires a Pug before he reaches that age should have him x-rayed at about ten months. Legg-Perthes can be corrected by surgery.

Luxating patella is a dislocation of the patella, the small, flat, moveable bone at the front of the knee. In mild cases the patella, which is held in place by ligaments, pops out of the groove in the femur in which it normally resides, then pops back in of its own accord. In severe cases the patella cannot return to its correct position on its own, and when it is manipulated into place, doesn't remain there long. A Pug with luxating patella favors his affected leg when he walks, and when he runs, he lifts it, setting it down only every few steps. The tendency to luxating patella is inherited, but excess weight can aggravate that tendency. Luxating patella can be corrected by surgery.

Pug dog encephalitis is an inflammation of the brain that is unique to Pugs. Its cause has not been identified. Seizure is the primary symptom of Pug dog encephalitis, which tends to affect young to middle-aged Pugs. Seizures are preceded sometimes by periods of lethargy and loss of muscle coordination. Other signs include agitation, aggression, pacing in circles, and pressing the head against objects.

Pugs with the slow, progressive form of encephalitis will return to normal between seizures, which recur in a few days or a few weeks. Pugs with the acute, rapidly progressing form of the disease walk abnormally and appear depressed and bewildered between seizures.

Phenobarbital helps to control seizures, corticosteroids help to reduce the inflammation of the brain, antibiotics can provide some relief if there is a bacterial component to the disease, but there is no cure for Pug dog encephalitis.

Progressive retinal atrophy (PRA) is the wasting away of the vessels in the retina, the innermost coat of the posterior part of the eyeball. PRA is manifested initially as night blindness in young dogs. As the disease progresses, its victims become totally blind.

Entropion is an inversion of the eyelid that usually affects the lower lid. Entropion, which can be corrected by surgery, causes persistent irritation of the cornea.

Pigmentary keratitis is the deposition of pigment or melanin on the surface of the eye by the cornea in response to unrelieved irritation and/or inflammation. Pigmentary keratitis is nature's way of telling Pug breeders they have gone too far in their quest for facial extremity, for as breeders have shortened the Pug's muzzle, they also have created the Pug's excessive nasal folds and shallow eye sockets. The latter cause the eyes to protrude, and if they protrude overmuch, the eyelids cannot fully cover and protect the cornea, nor can they distribute the tear film effectively over the entire surface of the eye. This condition is known as lagophthalmos, and it is one of the causes of prolapsed eyes and of dry eye or keratoconjunctivitis (KCS). Other irritating factors include ingrown eyelashes (trichiasis), aberrant eyelid hairs (distichiasis), and trauma to the eye.

Pigmentary keratitis can be permanent if the cause of the irritation or inflammation is not removed—by surgery if necessary—be it excessive nasal fold tissue, ingrown hairs, or KCS. After the cause of the problem has been eliminated, superficial deposits of pigment can be treated with topical eye medications. Pigment deep within the cornea may not be so easily treated, and if it impairs a Pug's vision, it should be removed surgically.

Elongated soft palate, which occurs in Pugs and other short-faced breeds like the Bulldog and the Pekingese, often results in some degree of obstruction of the dog's airway. This obstruction results in snorting, snoring, and breathing through the mouth. In severe cases of elongated palate, it partially blocks the opening into the voice box. If secondary changes in the voice box take place, acute airway obstruction may occur. If your Pug begins to honk like a goose, put his head back, and gasp for air, consult your veterinarian to see if he or she considers your Pug a candidate for the surgery necessary to correct an elongated soft palate.

Stenotic nares, a birth defect found in short-nosed breeds, is caused by nasal cartilage that is too soft. Stenotic nares, literally "narrow nostrils," collapse when a dog inhales. This prevents the dog from drawing in air. Dogs with this condition have a foamy-looking nasal discharge, and they breathe through their mouths when excited. Stenotic nares can be corrected surgically.

Several interpretations of what Swift might have had in mind when he said, "Every dog must have his day."

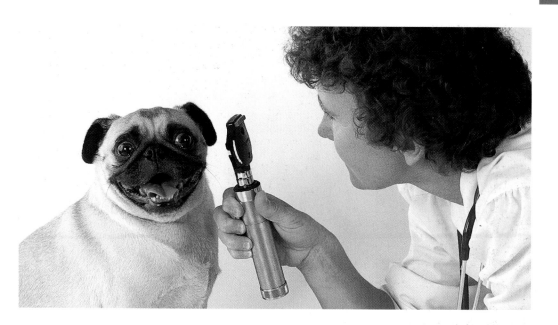

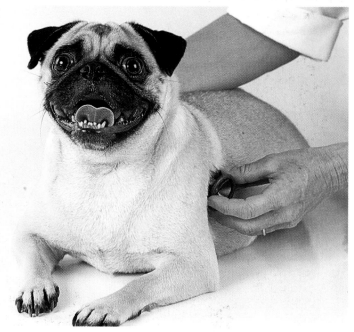

One of the many glories of living with Pugs is their virtual imperviousness to mishap. In nearly a decade of cohabitating with these charming dogs we have never had an emergency, unless you count the time we noticed that Burt was squinting one eye, so we took him to the veterinarian, who told us that Burt had a scratch on his cornea, and prescribed some medicine. This record has not been compiled because our dogs are house potatoes either. They spend large amounts of time in their fenced-in yard, and we often take them for rides in the van, which, ideally from the dogs' point of view, culminate in a run through a field somewhere. Understandably, then, our first-aid kit has always consisted of our veterinarian's phone number and a towel—both of which we always carry with us.

I hope that everyone who reads this book is as fortunate as we have been. In the event that you are not, however, or if your level of paranoia is higher than ours—or if you simply prefer traveling a little heavier than we do—here is a checklist of some first-aid items you may want

First-Aid Kit

- ✔ Blanket
- ✔ Gauze sponges
- ✔ Roll of narrow gauze
- ✔ Roll of bandages, such as a gauze wrap that stretches and clings
- ✔ Adhesive tape, hypo-allergenic
- ✔ Nonadherent sterile pads
- ✔ Small scissors
- ✔ Pediatric rectal thermometer
- ✔ Water-based sterile lubricant
- ✔ Three-percent hydrogen peroxide
- ✔ Rubbing alcohol
- ✔ Topical antibiotic ointment
- ✔ Epsom salts
- ✔ Baby-dose syringe or eye dropper (unbreakable)
- ✔ Sterile eye lubricant
- ✔ Sterile saline eye wash
- ✔ Styptic powder or pencil
- ✔ Petroleum jelly
- ✔ Your Pug's vital statistics (weight, age, preexisting conditions)
- ✔ A calm demeanor
- ✔ National Animal Poison Control Center telephone numbers (1-888-426-4435 or 1-900-680-0000). These calls are not toll-free.

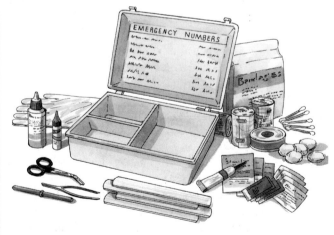

In case of emergency a first-aid kit can be a life saver.

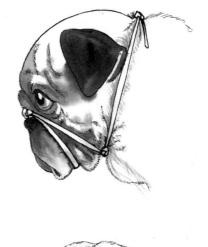

══ TIP ══

Heatstroke

Heatstroke, which occurs when rectal temperature spikes to 109.4°F (43°C) or when it lingers around 106°F (41°C), destroys cell membranes and leads to organ failures. The dehydration that accompanies heatstroke thickens the blood, thereby depriving tissues of necessary oxygen. The muscles, kidneys, liver, and gastrointestinal tract also may be affected. Moreover, heatstroke can cause swelling and subsequent damage to the brain, blindness, hemorrhages, convulsions, and fatal seizures.

If your Pug becomes overheated and pants excessively after being outdoors, take his temperature at once. If his temperature is elevated, give him some cold water to drink and then reduce his temperature slowly with a cold, but not icy cold, water bath.

An emergency muzzle may come in handy should misfortune befall your Pug.

to keep on hand. Many of these items may already be in your medicine cabinet or a kitchen drawer.

Fashioning an Emergency Muzzle

Should misfortune befall your Pug, do not contribute to it by dancing around hysterically and/or screeching in a high-pitched voice. Keep yourself and your dog calm, call the veterinarian, and follow his or her instructions scrupulously. If you're afraid your Pug may bite, fashion a muzzle from a strip of gauze. Tie a loose single knot in the center of the gauze and slide the loop over your Pug's muzzle in such a way that the knot is under your dog's chin—not always a simple job in a short-faced breed. Pull the loop until it fits snugly over the muzzle, then draw the ends of the gauze behind your Pug's ears and secure the makeshift muzzle with another single knot. If this contrivance remains in place, your dogs have longer faces than ours.

UNDERSTANDING YOUR PUG

There is no better company on two legs or four than a Pug dog. No friend is more loyal, no comrade more jolly, no confidant more trusty than this snuffling little bundle of *joie de vivre*. Pugs are willing to hold court in town or country. Their spirit can warm a drafty old mansion. Their simple requirements can be accommodated in the tiniest apartment. Fame, wealth, power, accomplishment, or social status make no difference to Pugs. Home is where the heart is, and their hearts are with their masters.

In addition to the unflagging companionship they provide, there are practical advantages to owning Pugs. They travel more easily and are accepted more readily in hotels or motels than are larger breeds. They will not eat a hole in your discretionary income. They do not require a lot of exercise. They can be washed quickly and allowed to drip dry, and best of all, because they are small, you can have more than one.

Pugs are good for us, and, supposedly, good for what ails us, too. They are always ready to assist at nap time, mealtime, bedtime, playtime, and all the other times of our lives. Pugs, indeed, are always time well spent. What's more, they are peerless at keeping secrets, accomplished at keeping us amused, and unrivaled at

The University of Pugonia synchronized dancing team practicing for the Super Bowl halftime show.

keeping loneliness from our doors. They have even been credited, along with other members of their species, with lowering our blood pressure, helping us to survive heart attacks and to stop smoking, and increasing our life spans.

Given a Pug's innumerable talents, the best reason for getting any Pug, is to enjoy the pleasures of his or her company, which pleasures are numerous. If you have never experienced the continuing joy of watching a Pug come to terms with the world, and trying to bend the world to its terms, your life is poorer for want of that experience. Pugs are all wide, soulful eyes, flapping, velvety ears, and panting enthusiasm. They are fetchingly soft, unerringly cute, endearingly klutzy, unfailingly energetic, and damnably stubborn on occasion. They can make you laugh when you do not have an inclination or a reason for doing so; they can coax a smile from your soul on the most grim, cheerless, lamentable days; and when the sun is shining, they have a way of looking at you as if it's shining only on you.

The lucky recipient of such companionship ought to be willing to return the same. If you do not enrich your Pug dog's life as much as he or she enriches yours, you are taking advantage of your Pug's good nature. That's a karmic transgression of the worst sort.

Your Pug will always be ready to lick your face when the muddy footprints of a frustrating day are stamped across your brow. When you are keyed up because of something the boss, the clerk at the convenience store, the person in the next cubicle at work, the president, some editorial writer, a loved one, the neighbor's kid, or someone on the Internet said or did recently, your Pug will be happy to sit and listen to you complain about the unfairness of it all. If you are a good Pug owner, you will be ready to return the favor. We should be just as willing to comfort Pugs for being dogs as they are to comfort us for being human.

Multum in Parvo

Such is the Pug's zest for living that the breed has been accorded its own motto: *Multum in parvo*, a Latin expression that means "a lot of dog in a small space." No one knows at what point in its 2,500-year history the Pug acquired this motto, but its author knew whereof he or she was speaking. The Pug dog is, indeed, larger than life.

A Pug gives you the convenience of a toy breed, the heart of a giant, the bravery of a terrier, the intelligence of a herding dog, and the face of a clown. Pugs are as loving, constant, and devoted as the day is long, as dependable as the sunrise. They are the best medicine when you are sick, an antidote to illness when you are well, and the greatest conversation starters on four feet. Most of the time the conversations begin favorably with some variation on the my-what-cute-little-dogs theme, but one chap, more candid than cautious, said to me outside a convenience store one day, "No offense, man, but those are some seriously ugly dogs." He was smiling, however, when he said it.

Comic Relief

A Pug is a punch line in search of a laugh. This dichotomy in fur possesses a body that looks like a cookie jar, and a gentle, jolly disposition belied by a face that appears as if its owner has just received tragic news. Thus, the more Pugs try to be serious, the funnier they become.

Our Pugs were seldom more amusing than when they tried to match strides with the Doberman next door. At least once a day his owners took him outside and threw or batted a ball for him to chase. The Doberman pursued the ball in graceful, loping strides—poetry in motion, a lesser writer might say.

Meanwhile, on their side of the chain link fence, our Pugs (we had four at the time) hurtled along helter-skelter, legs a-blur, eyes

Pugs have to run twice as fast as other dogs in order to go half as far.

Patty signals a left-hand turn while keeping her right foot on the steering wheel.

a-bulge, ears a-flapping. Our fence ends before the neighbor's yard does, and the Dobe had picked up the ball and loped back to his owner by the time our Pugs reached the end of the fence. Like characters in a cartoon, they put on the brakes, did a U-turn, spun their wheels for a split second before getting traction, and raced back to where the Doberman's owner had just hit the ball again. On went the brakes, the last Pug became first, and the Pugs were off again. If the Doberman's owner stopped to pet him before throwing the ball, our Pugs would start hopping up and down like auto-mated pogo sticks, barking their heads off, their loose skin piled like a dropped pair of drawers around their butts.

Soon after we had gotten our first Pugs, we stopped going to restaurants that did not have windows near which we could sit, the better to keep an eye on the dogs, who insist on going everywhere that we go and who look at us as though we were child abusers if we try to leave the house without them. One afternoon while I was enjoying a few slices of pizza and *The Spectator* in a local establishment, I heard a horn being sounded somewhat impatiently. A few seconds later I heard it again. Then again.

"I think your dogs are calling you," said the pizza shop owner's wife, who was fairly dou-bled over with laughter.

When I looked out the window, I saw why. There was Patty, front paws on the steering wheel of the minivan, looking for all the world like an irate driver stuck in some surrealistic traffic jam, her head bobbing up and down while she barked insults at the world. In the other front seat, equally frosted looking, sat her mother, Debbie, with a 1,000-yard glare on her face. When Patty finally stopped tooting the horn and the owner of the pizza shop finally stopped laughing, the minivan lights came on. It was time to go home.

Hans Goes Swimming

A few years ago when we had "only" five Pugs (we now have eight), we packed up and left for a few days in East Otis, Massachusetts, where my wife's parents have a summer place.

East Otis is in the foothills of the Berkshire mountains. It's the kind of place that can be seen only from the air. Some wags—especially those who enjoy a little nightlife, ethnic food, and cable television—have observed that from the air is the only way to see East Otis.

There is a reservoir, which everyone calls a lake, in East Otis. My wife's parents have a

"I don't care what you do to me, I'm not telling you where I hid your doggone bone."

cottage—two cottages, actually—on the lake. We repair to this compound several times during the summer. The company is superb, the surroundings tranquil (except for the occasional jet skier), and dogs are allowed. Indeed, I could not say who enjoys the lake more—Mary Ann and I or the Pugs—although they do grumble occasionally about the lack of good ethnic food.

The dogs all were curious about the lake at first, but none showed any interest in swimming, and all knew not to go too near the edges of the boat dock. The dock, roughly 12 feet (3.6 m)

Pugs love companionship, especially that of other Pugs.

Playtime for most Pugs begins shortly after they awake and ends shortly before they fall asleep.

music that serves as the soundtrack of our lives went dead. (What do you mean you don't hear music all the time?) Even though the interval between the time Hans went into a crouch and what he did next was less than a second, it seemed as though enough time had passed to drive to the fast-food trailer and back. For sure, his life flashed before my eyes.

wide and 25 feet (7.2 m) long, extends out over water about 4 feet (1.2 m) deep.

One Saturday morning in June, while the water temperature was still too low for swimming, we took the dogs walking by the lake. They had ventured onto the dock and were sniffing around when all of a sudden Hans, who was then our youngest, just six months old at the time, did one of those things that are so stupefying they send time screeching into slow motion.

I was standing on the dock gazing idly over the water contemplating a lunch-time visit across the lake to the fast-food trailer that sells clam bellies. Clam bellies, for the food impaired, are to clam strips what aged provolone is to cheese food. In New England, where the Cabots (or is it the Lodges?) speak only to God, everyone leaves the bellies on the clams, because God put them there for a reason: They taste good.

As I was saying, while I was contemplating bellying up at the fast-food trailer with the tourists, Hans went into a crouch. That is when time began to creep, as Shakespeare once said, in a "petty pace." That is also when the internal

What Hans did next was hurl himself in a perfect approximation of a belly flop straight out over the lake. We knew his vertical leap was impressive. We have the scratches on our kitchen door to prove it (no bad stifles on this boy), but we were not aware that his horizontal leap was equally impressive.

As soon as Hans had disappeared beneath the surface of the lake with a splendid *kerplash,* time did the weirdest thing. It went from s-l-o-w motion to *fastforward* in a rush. Without giving a thought to my personal safety, I yelled, "Quick, Hon, Hans jumped into the lake."

By that time Hans had turned around toward the dock. His little legs were churning the water purposefully, while his head floated on the surface like a huge muffin with two prunes for eyes. Hans, like many young Pugs, had a touch of the east-west eyes then, and the last thing I saw before his head went beneath the surface of the lake a second time were the whites of his eyes, which were sweeping the sky like searchlights.

Mary Ann rushed to the end of the dock and began to remove her watch. "Quick, Hon," I said. "He's going to drown."

*This Pug is taking a breather in the middle
of a serious discussion with a rawhide bagel.*

Forgetting about the watch, she jumped into
the lake. When she hit the water, she made the
kind of sound that someone in the shower
makes when someone else in the house turns
on the water in the kitchen and the water
in the shower drops 50 degrees in a second.
Only she made it louder. She also had this
look of quizzical apprehension on her face
that I had not seen since she approached
the altar the day we were married. Meanwhile, Hans had come back to the surface to
see what all the splashing was about. Mary
Ann lifted him up out of the water. I bravely
grabbed him and placed him on the dock.
(Later, friends of ours who own larger, more
athletic dogs said we need not have been so
worried. Hans would have made his way back
to shore. At the risk of sounding argumenta-
tive, I must say that it looked to me as if the
only thing he was making his way to was the
bottom of the lake. Perhaps he was planning to
walk ashore.)

When Mary Ann emerged from the lake, she
discovered that her watch was missing. The
lake water being quite clear, we were able to
make out the watch, a Timex, on the bottom
of the lake. Somebody would have to go back
into the frigid water.

Mary Ann changed from her sodden denim
jumper into her bathing suit, donned diving
glasses, and reentered Lake Hans. Five seconds
later she came up from underwater and

handed me her watch. I held it triumphantly
aloft and said, "See ladies and gentlemen, it
takes a soaking and keeps on stroking. Nothing
in the world beats a Timex."

The Bottom Line

Anyone writing a book about Pugs would
run out of space long before running out of
anecdotes, for Pugs are endlessly amusing.
Through the centuries they have been bred
for one purpose alone: to provide love and
companionship to a species that desperately
needs them. Pugs are good at their work, so
good, in fact, that an acquaintance of ours is
fond of saying, "A dog is a dog, but a Pug is
another person in your house." And what
good people they are. A house is not a home
without a Pug.

OBEDIENCE TRAINING

Despite their reputation for being single-minded—some would say stubborn—Pugs are apt and willing pupils, eager to please and able to learn. As your Pug's teacher you must bring the same cheerful, intelligent, resolute bearing to each training session. Because your patience will be tried and rewarded alternately while you are teaching your Pug to come, walk on a lead, sit, and stay, do not begin training if you are out of sorts. Leave the training for another day.

The Alpha Dog Principle

Basic training, which essentially consists of teaching your Pug where to conduct her personal affairs, should begin as soon as you acquire your dog. As this training progresses, she will learn that certain behaviors are met with praise. The satisfaction she gets from being praised, and her eagerness to please you, are the foundations on which later obedience training is built.

Dogs always have depended on the ability to function within a social hierarchy to survive, a dependence that leads them to seek our approval. In the wild—a concept that is difficult to entertain when it comes to Pugs—dogs and their wolfish ancestors lived in a hierarchy dominated by the alpha member, or leader, of the pack. The alpha dog, which generally is, contrary to popular misperception, a female, is judge,

If the eyes are the windows of the soul, then Pugs are all soul.

jury, sheriff, exalted ruler, and high priestess of the pack. When the alpha dog wants to rest, the other members of the pack lie down obligingly. When the alpha dog wants to move on, the pack follows. When the alpha dog wants to hunt, the pack members sharpen their fangs.

This centuries-old predisposition to function in a follow-the-leader arrangement makes it possible for you to assume the role of the alpha dog in your Pug's life. This principle also makes it possible for little, 18-pound (8.2-kg) dogs to dominate people who are seven, ten, or more than a dozen times their size—and who are often more intelligent to boot. Every pack must have a leader. If you do not want the job, your Pug will gladly take it. Before you allow this to happen, you should remember the old saying to the effect that if you ain't the lead dog, the scenery seldom changes.

What's in a Name?

Some Pug owners spend considerable time choosing their Pugs' names. Other owners let names evolve out of the warp and woof of daily living. The latter kind of person usually has a dog named Trashmaster or Peabrain. Dogs belonging to people for whom names are a serious business usually answer to things like Waterford or Lord Halversham.

Our first Pug, whom we acquired when he was nine months old, had been named Percy before we got him. Because we live in a small town where anyone who goes out into the

TRAINING TIPS

1 Keep training sessions brief: five minutes or so at a time in the beginning. Two five-minute sessions a day are better than a single ten-minute session.

2 Conduct training sessions in the same location with the same unfailing patience each time. After your Pug has mastered a command, you can vary the setting to see if that learning is transferable.

3 Reward your Pug with praise and the occasional treat when she does well. If she associates performance with good feelings, she will be more likely to perform willingly.

4 Do not use your Pug's name to scold her if she makes a mistake during training. In fact, do not scold her at all during training. When she makes a mistake, show her by voice and example what you want her to do.

5 Limit your Pug to one teacher. Different folks have different strokes when it comes to interacting with dogs. This might be fine sociologically, but it plays havoc with the training experience.

6 If your Pug attempts to leave before a training session is over, bring her back quietly and try again. Do not call her by name when you are trying to coax her back to the training site, or she'll be loathe to come again when she is called.

7 Do not let the session end unless you are ready to end it.

8 If you are practicing indoors, have a lead handy in case the doorbell rings and you have to go and answer it in the middle of a training session. Put the lead on your Pug and walk her to the door, then send the person away and go back to your training session. Of course, you will not have to bother answering the phone during a training session. That's why answering machines were invented.

9 Let other members of the household know that you do not wish to be disturbed during a training session.

10 If your Pug is not catching on to a lesson as quickly as you would like, ask yourself what you are doing wrong. Are you going too quickly? Are you handling her too abruptly? Has an impatient tone infiltrated your voice? Are you rewarding her as soon as she does the right thing? Is it time to take a step back and go over a routine she already knows for a few days in order to build up her confidence before coming back to the lesson that's giving her trouble?

backyard and yells "Percy, come" at a small dog is liable to attract unfavorable attention from Peabrain's owners, we had planned to change Percy's name to something less conspicuous. Alas, by the time Percy arrived at our house, he had become attached to his name. His name being the only thing he had brought with him from his former home, we decided not to change it.

If your Pug, no matter how old she is when you acquire her, has a name and knows what it is, we suggest you keep that name. You may shorten it some, if possible, for public consumption—from *Percy* to *Perc* with a soft *c*, for example—but your Pug will have enough to do adjusting to a new home without having to adjust to a new identity as well.

If your Pug has not been named by her breeder, or if she has not yet learned her name, you can teach her to respond to whatever name you want her to respond to by rewarding her with extravagant praise every time she does. Like humans, dogs consider the sound of their names the world's sweetest music, and if that sound is associated with great praise, your Pug will learn to respond to her name in short order.

Suppose, for example, you have decided to name your Pug Bridget. While you are playing with her, or sitting quietly with her for that matter, pronounce her name with a certain high-pitched, ascending gusto. If she looks in any direction but yours, do nothing. Wait a second or two, and say her name again. Unless she is stone deaf, Bridget will look toward you eventually. When she does, say "Good" and reward her with pats, hugs, and kisses.

You now have Bridget's attention. Wait a minute or two and say her name again. You may have to say it two or even three times, but if you put enough excitement into your tone, Bridget will look at you eventually. When she does, make a fuss over her again. After she has responded to her name three or four times in one session, you have accomplished your mission. If you repeat that mission two or three times a day for a week or so, you will have Bridget's ear any time you call her name, and she will come to realize that the sound of those two syllables has a special meaning all its own.

Useful Commands

Come

The first command you should teach your Pug is to come when she is called. Once she has learned to respond to a vocal summons virtually without fail or insubordination, you will have established a significant measure of control over her, a control that could serve her well in times of trouble. What's more, the confidence you will have acquired in teaching your Pug to come when you call will give you more confidence in teaching her additional commands.

Step one: If Bridget is responding well to her name, teaching her to come when you call should not be difficult. Many dogs begin loitering in the kitchen well before mealtime. When they see the food bowl descending toward the floor, they zoom toward it instantly. You can make this tendency work to your advantage by saying *"Bridget, come"* before moving the bowl from the kitchen counter to the floor. You could use *here* or any other word instead of *come* when you wish to summon Bridget, but once you have chosen a call word, use it exclusively. It does not matter how old Bridget is when you begin this routine, but the best time to begin it is right after she has learned to respond to her name.

In addition to rewarding Bridget with her meal for coming when you call, be sure to add a lavish helping of praise before you set the bowl down. This will reinforce the behavior you desire because Bridget will associate the word *come* with food and praise.

Some dogs do not appear in the kitchen until they hear the rattle of the dry food container, the sound of a can being opened, or the squeak of the drawer where the can opener lives. If Bridget is one of those dogs, say *"Bridget, come"* before doing any of these guaranteed-to-get-her-attention activities.

Step two: After two or three weeks you will have "trained" Bridget to come when you call, at mealtimes, but there will be other times of the day and other parts of the house where you will want her to answer this command readily. Begin this second phase of training— it will be the first phase for those rare dogs that do not race to the kitchen at the sound of the can opener—in a room from which there is no escape and no foolproof place for Bridget to hide. Wander into that room with a few of Bridget's favorite treats in your pocket. If Bridget begins to come over to greet you, say *"Bridget, come"* and take a treat out of your pocket. As soon as she is close enough to get the treat, say *"Good"* in a high-pitched, happy tone and reward her with the treat.

Should Bridget appear more interested in what she was doing before you came in than in coming over to greet you, move casually to a spot about 2 or 3 feet (61–91 cm) from her.

According to the American Kennel Club standard, the pug's "symmetry and general appearance are decidedly square and cobby."

The defense attorney huddles with his client during a pause in the trial.

Say *"Bridget, come,"* then offer her the treat. If she comes to you, say *"Good"* and give her the treat. If she ignores you, reach over quietly, pick her up, move her to you, praise her with pats and a hug—but not with the word *good*—and give her the treat. Save *good* for those occasions when she has done the requested action.

Praising a dog that just has ignored you might seem unwise, but you would be even less wise to allow Bridget to ignore you when she pleases. By picking Bridget up and moving her to the place where you want her to be, you are teaching her that she is either going to come when she is called or you are going to see that she does.

After Bridget has complied with the *come* command two or three times, willingly or by proxy, end the lesson. In this as in all other lessons, never end the lesson on a disobedient note. The last request you make of your dog must be obeyed, even if you have to simulate obedience by carrying or walking her through the command.

Step three: Once Bridget begins to respond regularly to the *come* command, do not give her a food reward every time she comes when you call. If she knows she can get a treat every time, she may decide on occasion that it is more rewarding to continue what she was doing, even if she was doing nothing, than to get that old predictable treat; but if she does not get a treat every time, she will not be certain that treats

Intermittent Reinforcement

Psychologists call the maybe-yes, maybe-no technique *intermittent reinforcement.* They caution, however, that the schedule of intermittent reinforcement must not be predictable. If you withhold the treat every third time you summon Bridget, she will soon glom on to that fact and begin timing her refusals to coincide with the empty hand. To be effective, intermittent reinforcement must be random. If your training sessions consist of four or five practices of the *come* command during two or three sessions a day, withhold the treat the second time you call Bridget during the first session, the fourth time during the second session, and so on.

Do not be intermittent with your praise, however. You do not want Bridget thinking that you love her less for some performances than for others. Every time she comes when you call, say *"Good,"* even if you do not give her a treat.

Bridget has answered your call three or four times. After Bridget is coming to you consistently when you call, increase the distance between you and her by gradual increments: first, to 4 or 5 feet (1.22–1.5 m) for several days and then to 6 or 7 feet (1.5–2.1 m) for several days. Keep increasing the distance between you and her until she responds to your command from across the room.

Finally, if you want to impress yourself, call her from the next room. For obvious reasons, the best room for you to be in when you first attempt this feat is the kitchen; and the best thing to do right after you call her, providing she is an only child, is to rattle a box of dry food. If you have other dogs, the sound of the dry food box might draw a crowd, which would be counterproductive. Either put them in the yard when you're training Bridget or rely on your seductive voice alone.

After Bridget is bounding regularly into the kitchen in response to the dry food box, call her without shaking the box, and give her copious applause and a treat when she comes running. Then, after she is racing to the kitchen in response to your voice alone, try calling her from other rooms in the house. If necessary, use the dry food box as an auxiliary training aid at first.

If at any point Bridget does not respond to your vocal summons from another room, do not make an issue of it and do not repeat the command. Perhaps she didn't hear you, and even if she did, the worst conclusion she will reach is that she can ignore you on occasion when you are not in the same room as she. Even in that event you will still be miles ahead of the game. Many dogs figure they can ignore their owners from any distance any time they choose.

are always forthcoming. Thus, she will be more likely to answer every time because she always will be hoping, as the old joke goes, that tonight is the night. This technique is known as intermittent reinforcement (see Tip).

Repeat the *come* exercise a few times a day, limiting the distance Bridget has to travel to 3 or 4 feet (.91–1.22 m) and restricting each session to two or three minutes in which

If your dog is colossally inflexible and refuses to come when you call—and if you are just as inflexible in your desire to teach her to respond to this command—put a harness or collar on her and attach the 6-foot (1.8-m) training lead to it. Then say, *"Bridget, come,"* and tug gently and briefly on the lead. If she does not respond to the call-tug summons, call her again and tug on the lead. If there is still no answer, pick her up and carry her to the spot from which you summoned her. Praise her lavishly but do not give her a treat. Then dismiss the class. Until she begins answering to *"Bridget, come"* with no more prompting than a short tug on the lead, you must end every lesson by carrying her into base.

Eventually, Bridget should begin responding to the *come* command with little more than a gentle tug on the lead by way of spiritual guidance. This is your signal to eliminate the tug after you have called her. If she responds to your voice only, her reward should be prodigious. If she is not yet voice-activated, revert to tugging on the lead as a means of inspiring her to come when called.

Be careful not to allow the use of the lead to degenerate into a tug-of-war. If Bridget digs in her heels and refuses to budge, walk over to her, pick her up gently, and move her to the spot from which you first called her.

When that glorious day on which Bridget comes to you in response to your voice alone finally dawns, bask in the glory of several more of those days. Then try the exercise without the benefit of the lead. If Bridget ignores you, go back to the lead.

From your Pug's point of view, there are only two reasons for coming when she is called: praise and food. Therefore, when you are training her to come when she is called, she always expects to be happy that she responded. Consequently, you never should call her when you want to give her medication, reprimand her, or do anything else that might cause her discomfort. If she associates a summons with an unpleasant consequence, she will begin ignoring all summonses.

After Bridget has learned to come faithfully when you call, you can reduce the lavish praise to a simple *"Good girl"* or a pat on the head by way of intermittent reinforcement. Do not eliminate the reinforcement altogether or you risk eliminating her willing response.

Sit

Teaching your Pug to sit on command evolves easily as an extension of lead training (see HOW-TO: Using a Collar, Harness, and Lead, page 86). After walking several paces with Bridget on a lead at your left, stop, and switch the lead to your right hand. Position your right hand above her head, say *"Sit,"* and pull up lightly on the lead. At the same time, place your left hand on her rump and press down gently but firmly. Once she sits down, praise her quietly, but control your enthusiasm. You want her to remain sitting. If she stands up, repeat the *sit* command. If you use a food reward in teaching this command, present it below your Pug's nose so that she can reach down for it without leaving the sitting position.

Once Bridget has been sitting for a few seconds, say *"Bridget, come"* and continue walking. After several paces, repeat the *sit* command. Do this another two or three times and end the lesson.

As you repeat the *sit* command on subsequent days, Bridget should need less and less prompting from the touch of the lead on her

neck and your hand on her rump. She has mastered the *sit* command when she can come to a stop and sit promptly when she hears the word *sit* while walking on a lead. At this point you do not have to transfer the lead from your left hand to your right any longer.

After your Pug has mastered the *sit* command on a lead, you and she can practice that exercise around the house. Call her to you and when she responds, say *"Bridget, sit."* If she hesitates, press down gently on her rump until she does, then praise her and give her a reward.

Stay

To teach the *stay* command, put your Pug in a sitting position on your left. With the lead in your left hand, lean down and place your right hand—palm toward your dog—about 6 inches (15 cm) in front of her face. Say *"Stay"* and, after you do, move slowly until you are facing your puppy from a distance of 2 or 3

There is nothing sweeter than the sound of a dog's name, especially when the person saying the name has a treat in hand.

feet (.61–.91 cm). The lead still will be in your left hand at this point, so if Bridget begins to move toward you, repeat the *stay* command and pull the lead straight up gently.

After your Pug has remained in position for five seconds or so, release her by calling her to you. Praise her and give her a treat if you wish, then take up the lead, walk several paces, tell her to sit, and once she does, repeat the *stay* command. Practice this command three or four more times before you end the lesson. As you practice the *stay* command on subsequent days, slowly increase the amount of time Bridget stays in place before you release her. Once she begins to master the command, you can practice it indoors. You can practice it while she is standing, too. As the practice sessions

Obedience training is the art of making a dog think that sitting, staying, etc. are his ideas not yours.

you and your Pug to 10 yards (9.1 m). Then, instead of giving the *stay* command and backing away from her, give the command, turn around, walk 10 paces, then turn and face her. If she has learned her lessons well, she ought to be sitting obediently in place. If she has followed you instead, repeat the exercise; but this time, after giving the *stay* command, walk only one or two steps before turning and facing your Pug.

continue, you will not need to reinforce the *stay* command by placing your hand in front of her face every time you issue the command.

When Bridget has mastered the *stay* command, you can begin to increase the distance between you and her while she is staying in place. Tell her to stay, set the lead on the ground, and take a small step or two backward. Repeat the *stay* command with the raised-hand signal for reinforcement if your Pug looks as if she is about to move. Return her to the sitting position if she does move. After she has stayed in place for ten or fifteen seconds or however long you want her to remain in place, release her and praise her for being a good dog.

During the course of several training sessions, gradually increase the distance between

HOW-TO: USING A COLLAR,

The Collar

Introduce your puppy to a collar by putting one around her neck just before you feed her. Remove the collar after she has eaten but before you take her outside for her post-meal walk. After a few days, put the collar on her at other times during the day. Leave it on for a little longer each time. We usually make this gradual introduction to the collar sometime after a puppy is twelve weeks old.

After a puppy has gotten used to wearing a collar—this shouldn't take more than a few days—add her identification tag and license tag to the collar. Our Pugs do not wear collars in the house or when they are in the yard barking insults at the neighbors, but a Pug should wear a collar whenever she leaves her property.

The Harness

Introducing a harness to your Pug is scarcely more complicated than introducing a collar. After spending a few minutes playing with and petting your Pug, set the harness on her back. At this point Pug owners are of two minds regarding procedure. One mind says to attach the harness right away; the other mind says to let it lie on your Pug's back a few seconds a day for several days before attaching it fully. The method you choose will depend on your Pug's reaction to the harness. If she recoils in disapproval, pet her a few seconds, remove the harness tenderly, and try again tomorrow. If she does not seem to mind the harness, you might as well hook it up and be done with it. Be sure to give her a treat once the harness is in place. Do not give her a treat if she recoils from the harness. Reassurance is enough in that case.

After your Pug consents to wearing the harness—which consent may be preceded by a period of rolling, scratching at the harness, and complaining—leave the harness on for five or ten minutes a day for several days, then leave it on for ten or fifteen minutes a day and, finally, for fifteen to twenty minutes a day after that.

When your Pug must be under control, your Pug should be in a collar or a harness.

Lead Training

Step 1: The lead should be added to the collar or harness in much the same way the collar and harness were added to your Pug—gradually. The first time you put the lead on your Pug, allow her to drag it around a few minutes and give her one or two treats during that interlude, then remove the lead. Repeat this routine for two or three days.

Step 2: Once your Pug is comfortable with the lead, pick up one end and hold it. Do not try to lead her anywhere; simply hold the lead while she moves about, following her wherever she goes. Remove the lead after three or four minutes.

Step 3: Now you are ready to have your Pug follow where you lead. To accomplish this she ought to be on your left side, facing the same direction that you are. Your right arm should be held naturally by your side, and the lead should be in your left hand. Show your dog the treat you have in your right hand, and take a step or two forward. If she steps forward, too—which she most certainly should—move a few additional steps forward. If she steps forward again, give her the treat. If she is reluctant to move, do not drag her. Show her the food again, this time holding it a little closer to her face. As soon as she moves toward it, say "Good," give her the food, and praise her for moving. If she refuses to move, pick her up, set her down a few paces forward, praise her for being a wonderful dog, but do not give her the treat. Then end the lesson for the day.

All tacked up and ready to go.

Your Pug should be willing to move a few steps the first day you have her on a lead. On subsequent days, increase the distance she must walk alongside you before she gets her treat.

Lead-training 101 should be conducted in your driveway or backyard. Do not try a public thoroughfare until your Pug walks attentively at your side.

Like any new lesson you present to your Pug, lead-training should be taught with large patience in small steps. New experiences can be unsettling for any animal. The easier you make the lesson, therefore, the more likely your Pug is to grasp it readily. Remember that pleasing you is one of the most pleasing activities for your Pug. Do not let your training methods put roadblocks on her path to happiness.

FUN AND GAMES

Are weekends no longer the carefree revels they used to be? Has the wind gone out of the yard sales? Have flea markets lost their bite? Is the local nature center for the birds? Are you a no-show at art, craft, and flower shows these days? Do museums seem more like mausoleums? Have you shopped until you dropped one too many bundles? Are you weary of those dowdy chefs who mince, dice, slice, and sauté the weekend long? Are you adrift from Friday until Monday because all the interesting support groups meet during the week?

If that's what's curdling your café latte, my friend, allow me to present the most splendid diversion of them all: the dog show, a glorious, intoxicating ritual that is equal parts religion, social gathering, art form, therapeutic exercise, and full-tilt shopping extravaganza all rolled, crimped, primped, styled, trimmed, trained, fluffed-up, combed-down, and blow-dried into one gosh-almighty affair.

Where the Shows Are

Dogs shows celebrate the unique bond that exists between people and dogs, and there is much to see and to experience at these celebrations: breathtaking dogs in dazzling display, vendors who offer the finest in canine accessories, boutiques that overflow with people

Stacking consists of positioning a dog to accentuate its good qualities while minimizing its deficiencies.

gifts for you or your dog-loving friends, and food stands in case all that shopping makes you hungry.

Before you start checking on your credit card balances, you will need to find a dog show to attend. The American Kennel Club can help in that regard by providing a list of the clubs in your area (see Information, page 92.)

Call the clubs near you and ask when their shows are going to be held and how many vendors will be on hand. Some shows have only a few vendors selling basic dog-care products; others are veritable shopping malls. The person to whom you speak can also tell you whether there is an admission charge for the show.

A Ringside Seat

When you arrive at a dog show, so much will be going on that you may feel as if you had begun watching a two-hour mystery on television one hour after it had started. Most shows draw at least 1,000 entries, and the larger shows attract as many as 2,500 dogs, sometimes more. The majority of those dogs compete in conformation classes for points toward their championships and/or for best of breed, group, and best in show. Winners are chosen in an altogether subjective manner by judges who evaluate each dog according to the written standard for its breed.

It would be impossible for any judge, even Judge Wapner, to evaluate that many dogs one after the other and then to select the winners. Therefore, a number of judges are hired for the task—a dozen or so, maybe more—and the task is simplified by having those judges work in separate rings simultaneously.

Every dog entered in a show is judged first against other members of its breed. Although the AKC recognizes 146 breeds, shows rarely have representatives of every breed in competition. There will be, however, 100 different breeds or more represented at most shows. Some of the rarer breeds may have only one or two entries, while more popular breeds may have thirty, forty, fifty or more dogs in competition.

Breed judging begins at 8:00 or 8:30 in the morning and lasts until mid-afternoon. All dogs entered in the show are judged initially against other members of their respective breeds. In this individual breed judging, the dogs that are not champions are judged first, and these are evaluated according to sex— males, which are called "dogs," precede females, which are called "bitches."

Nonchampion dogs or bitches may be entered in one of five classes: puppy, novice, bred by exhibitor, American bred, and open. There are strategic reasons for choosing the class in which to enter a dog, but those reasons need not concern or confuse us here.

After the classes of males have been judged, the first-place dogs from each class compete in

the winners class. The winner of that class, the winner's dog, is awarded points toward its championship. The judging process that resulted in the selection of the winner's dog is then repeated for the bitches in a breed. A dog or a bitch must earn fifteen points to become a champion. Those points can be earned one, two, three, four, or five at a time, depending on the number of other entries a dog or a bitch defeats in a particular day's competition.

After the winner's bitch has been selected, she, the winner's dog, and any champions that have been entered in the show compete in the best-of-breed class. The winner of that class and its owner and/or handler get to hang around until mid-afternoon when they compete in group judging.

The 146 breeds recognized by the AKC are divided into seven groups—sporting, hound, working, terrier, toy, nonsporting, and herding— according to the purpose for which a breed was created. Dogs that hunt birds (pointers, setters, retrievers, spaniels, and others) belong to the sporting group. Dogs that hunt animals by sight or scent (Afghans, Borzois, Bassets, and so on) belong to the hound group. Dogs that pull sleds or carts (Siberian Huskies, for example) or perform rescue work (Newfoundlands or St. Bernards) or draw guard duty (Mastiffs, Rottweilers, and so forth) belong to the working group. Dogs that go to earth to roust badgers, foxes, or other creatures belong to the terrier group. Dogs whose sole function is to provide companionship (Pugs, Pekingese, Toy Poodles, Chihuahuas, and others) are members of the toy group. Dogs that seem to defy categorization (Standard Poodles, Bulldogs, Dalmatians, Lhasa Apsos, and so on) are assigned to the nonsporting group. Dogs that herd flocks (German Shepherd dogs, Shetland

> "They all had a free and glorious life, and your own is sweetened by the certainty you have brought only unconfined delight to a creature whose existence wags and spins on your love and approval."
> —John Osborne, *The Spectator*
> 7 May 1994

Sheep Dogs, Australian Cattle Dogs, and others) belong to the herding group.

Unlike breed judging, in which dozens of breeds may be judged at the same time, group judging is generally conducted one or at the most two groups at a time. After the seven group winners have been selected, they return for one more appraisal—the best-in-show competition. The winner from that elite group is the day's top dog.

Obedience Competition

Of all the signs and wonders to be seen at a dog show, the most wondrous occur in the obedience rings. There, dogs of various sizes, shapes, and descriptions heed verbal and visual commands as if they (the dogs) were electronically controlled robots in fur. The handler walks forward; the dog walks obligingly at his or her left side. The handler stops; the dog comes to an immediate halt, then sits promptly to await further instruction. The handler tosses an object; the dog remains seated until he is told to move, then retrieves the object and trots back to the handler.

In obedience classes dogs also jump, lie down, and hold that thought on command. They pick out from a group of objects the one object that a handler has touched, ignoring the objects that do not bear the handler's scent the way a preppy ignores polyester. In one exercise sure to confound any schoolteacher who has stepped out of a classroom momentarily only to discover upon returning that three felonies have been committed in her absence, a group of handlers instructs their dogs to lie down, tells them to stay in that position, then leaves the vicinity for more

> "People often accuse them [Pugs] of being child substitutes, but I reckon it's the other way round. Women have children only when they aren't lucky enough to have a Pug."
>
> Anonymous Pug Owner

time than it takes to get a divorce in some states. When the handlers return, their dogs are sitting precisely where they were left, with serene, butter-wouldn't-melt expressions on their faces.

Vendors

A dog show, as we have noted, is more than simply a place to show dogs. It is a dog lover's dream-of-a-lifetime shopping spree come true. The vendors' booths on the show grounds offer the finest in dog food and vitamins; water bowls and feeding dishes; dog-proof carriers, crates, and exercise pens; beds, combs, brushes, powders, shampoos, and other grooming aids; attractive toys; and lots of people merchandise, too. The latter includes but is by no means limited to jewelry, T-shirts, sweatshirts, posters, and other accessories.

Extracurricular Activities

Pug owners needn't enter their dogs in shows in order to meet and greet other Pug lovers. There are a number of social gatherings across the country at which every Pug is a guaranteed winner. Consult your telephone book, the newspaper, and Information on page 92 of this book to see if there's a Pug lovers club near you. And if there isn't, why not start one of your own?

International Kennel Clubs

American Kennel Club
260 Madison Avenue
New York, NY 10016
Tel: (212) 696-8200

Canadian Kennel Club
2150 Bloor Street West
Toronto, Ontario
M6S 4VT
Canada

The Kennel Club
1-4 Clargis Street
Picadilly, London
W1Y 8AB
England

National Breed Club

Pug Dog Club of America*

National Lost Pet Registries

National Dog Registry
P.O. Box 118
Woodstock, NY 12498-0116
Tel: (800) 637-3647

Petfinders
368 High Street
Athol, NY 12810
Tel: (800) 223-4747

Tattoo-A-Pet
1625 Emmons Avenue
Brooklyn, NY 11235
Tel: (800) TATTOOS

Animal Protection Organizations

American Humane Association
P.O. Box 1266
Denver, CO 80201
Tel: (303) 695-0811

American Society for the Prevention
of Cruelty to Animals (ASPCA)
441 East 92nd Street
New York, NY 10028
Tel: (212) 876-7700

Friends of Animals
P.O. Box 1244
Norwalk, CT 06856
Tel: (800) 631-2212

Periodicals

Dog Fancy
P.O. Box 53264
Boulder, CO 80322
Tel: (303) 786-7306

Dog and Kennel
7-L Dundas Circle
Greensboro, NC 27407
Tel: (336) 292-4047

Dog World
29 North Wacker Drive
Chicago, IL 60606
Tel: (312) 726-2802

Pug Talk
5037 Plover Road
Wise Rapids, WI 54494
Subscription rate: $30 annually for 6 issues

---

*To obtain the name and address of the current
club secretary, inquire at the American Kennel
Club (212) 696-8200 or visit the club's web site
at *www.pugs.org*

The Happa Pug, an ancient breed that's half Pug and half statue.

Books

Alderton, David. *The Dog Care Manual.* Hauppauge, NY: Barron's Educational Series, Inc., 1986.

Baer, Ted. *Communicating With Your Dog,* 2nd Edition. Hauppauge, NY: Barron's Educational Series, Inc., 1999.

Carlson, Delbert G., D.V.M., and James Griffin, M.D. *Dog Owner's Home Veterinary Handbook,* New York, NY: Howell Book House, 1980.

Klever, Ulrich. *The Complete Book of Dog Care.* Hauppauge, NY: Barron's Educational Series, Inc., 1989.

Pinney, Chris C. *Guide to Home Pet Grooming.* Hauppauge, NY: Barron's Educational Series, Inc., 1990.

Thomas, Shirley. *The New Pug.* New York, NY: Howell Book House, 1990.

Wrede, Barbara. *Civilizing Your Puppy,* 2nd Edition. Hauppauge, NY: Barron's Educational Series, Inc., 1997.

About the Author

Phil Maggitti is a freelance writer and editor living happily ever after in southeastern Pennsylvania with his wife Mary Ann, eight Pug dogs and seven cats. Mr. Maggitti has received a number of awards for his writing, including two awards from the American Horse Council—for best feature article in 1985 and for best personal column in 1986—and one award from the Dog Writers Association of America for best single-breed booklet in 1994.

Other Barron's titles by Phil Maggitti:
Birman Cats: A Complete Pet Owner's Manual (1996)
Before You Buy That Kitten (1995)
Guide to a Well-Behaved Cat (1993)
Scottish Fold Cats: A Complete Pet Owner's Manual (1993)

Photo Credits

Norvia Behling: pages 3, 16, 20 left, 29 bottom, 32, 33 top, 40, 41, 49, 56, 61, 64 bottom right, 65, 80, 84, 85; Isabelle Francais: pages 4, 8 bottom, 9, 17 top, 24, 33 bottom, 73 top, 76, 81; Bonnie Nance: pages 8 top, 64 top; Jean Wentworth: page 72; Zig Lesczcynski: pages 12, 20 right; Kent and Donna Dannen: pages 17 bottom, 57, 64 bottom left, 88, 93; Toni Tucker: pages 21, 36, 44, 60; Aaron Norman: pages 28, 29 top; Pets by Paulette: page 48; Phil Maggitti: page 73 bottom.

Cover Credits

Pets by Paulette

Important Note

This book is concerned with selecting, keeping, and raising Pugs. The publisher and the author think it is important to point out that the advice and information for Pug maintenance applies to healthy, normally developed animals. Anyone who acquires an adult dog or one from an animal shelter must consider that the animal may have behavioral problems and may, for example, bite without any visible provocation. Such anxiety biters are dangerous for the owner as well as the general public.

Caution is further advised in the association of children with dogs, in meetings with other dogs, and in exercising the dog without a leash.

All inquiries should be addressed to:
Barron's Educational Series, Inc.
250 Wireless Boulevard
Hauppauge, NY 11788
http://www.barronseduc.com

International Standard Book No. 0-7641-1045-4

Library of Congress Catalog Card No. 99-40285

Library of Congress Cataloging-in-Publication Data
Maggitti, Phil.
  Pugs : everything about purchase, care, nutrition, breeding, behavior, and training / Phil Maggitti : drawings by Michele Earle-Bridges.—2nd ed.
    p. cm. — (A complete pet owner's manual)
  Includes bibliographical references (p.) and index.
  ISBN 0-7641-1045-4 (alk. paper)
  1. Pug. I. Title. II. Series.
SF429.P9M34   2000
636.76—dc21   99-40285
                                         CIP

Printed in Hong Kong

9 8 7 6